P9-DEW-552

A HISTORY OF
MULTICULTURAL AMERICA

The New Freedom
to the New Deal
1913-1939

William Loren Katz

RSVP

**RAINTREE
STECK-VAUGHN**
P U B L I S H E R S
The Steck-Vaughn Company

Austin, Texas

For Laurie

Cover and interior design: Joyce Spicer
Electronic Production: Scott Melcer

Library of Congress Cataloging-in-Publication Data

Katz, William Loren.
    The new freedom to the New Deal, 1913-1939 / by William Loren Katz.
       p.   cm. — (A History of multicultural America)
    Includes bibliographical references and index.
    Summary: A multicultural history of the United States, from 1913 to 1939, focusing on the experiences of women and minorities.
    ISBN 0-8114-6279-X   —   ISBN 0-8114-2916-4 (soft cover)
    1. United States — History — 1913-1921 — Juvenile literature.
2. United States — History — 1919-1933 — Juvenile literature.
3. United States — History — 1933-1945 — Juvenile literature.
[1. United States — History — 1913-1921   2. United States — History — 1919-1933   3. United States — History — 1933-1945
4. Minorities — History.   5. Women — History.]   I. Title.
II. Series: Katz, William Loren. History of multicultural America.
E766.K3   1993
973.91—dc20   92-39948
                                                  CIP
                                                  AC

Printed and bound in the United States of America

3 4 5 6 7 8 9 0 LB 98 97 96 95 94

Acknowledgments

All prints from the collection of the author, William L. Katz with the following exceptions: pp. 22, 26, 27, 29, 33 (both), 74 The Bettmann Archive; pp. 17, 23 (both), 24b, 38, 49, 84 The Library of Congress; p. 28b New York Daily News; p. 41 Tamiment Library, New York University; p. 45 The Sophia Smith Collection; p. 47 New York State Library; p. 85c AP/Wide World.

Cover photographs: (inset) The Granger Collection; (map) Courtesy UCLA Map Library.

TABLE OF CONTENTS

INTRODUCTION

The history of the United States is the story of people of many backgrounds. A few became wealthy through their knowledge of science, industry, or banking. But it was ordinary people who most shaped the progress of this country and created our national heritage.

The American experience, however, has often been recounted in history books as the saga of powerful men—presidents and senators, merchants and industrialists. Schoolchildren were taught that the wisdom and patriotism of an elite created democracy and prosperity.

A truthful history of the United States has to do more than celebrate the contributions of the few. Ordinary Americans fought the Revolution that set this country free, and ordinary workers built the nation's economy. The overwhelming majority of people held no office, made little money, and worked hard all their lives.

Some groups, women and minorities in particular, had to vault legal barriers and public hostility in order to make their contributions to the American dream, only to find that school courses taught little about their achievements. The valiant struggle of minorities and women to win dignity, equality, and justice often was omitted from history's account. Some believe this omission was accidental or careless, others insist it was purposeful.

Native Americans struggled valiantly to survive military and cultural assaults on their lives. But the public was told Native Americans were savages undeserving of any rights to their land or culture. African Americans battled to break the chains of slavery and to scale the walls of racial discrimination. But a century after slavery ended, some textbooks still pictured African Americans as content under slavery and bewildered by freedom. Arrivals from Asia, Mexico, and the West Indies faced legal restrictions and sometimes violence. But the public was told that they were undeserving of a welcome because they took "American jobs," and some were "treacherous aliens."

Whether single, married, or mothers, women were portrayed as dependent on men and accepting of a lowly status. The record of their sturdy labors, enduring strengths, and their arduous struggle to achieve equality rarely found its way into classrooms. The version of American history that reached the public carried many prejudices. It often preferred farmers over urban workers, middle classes over working classes, rich over poor. Women and minorities became invisible, ineffective, or voiceless.

This distorted legacy also failed to mention the campaigns waged by minorities and women to attain human rights. Such efforts did not reflect glory on white male rulers and their unwillingness to extend democracy and opportunity to others.

This kind of history was not a trustworthy tale. It locked out entire races and impeded racial understanding. Not only was it unreliable, but for most students it was dull and boring.

Our history has to be truthful and complete. Our struggle to overcome the barriers of nature and obstacles made by humans is an inspiring story. This series of books seeks to explore the heroic efforts of minorities and women to find their place in the American dream.

William Loren Katz

CHAPTER 1

PRESIDENT WILSON AND AMERICANIZATION

The years of the two presidential terms of Woodrow Wilson (1913-1921) brought enormous changes to American ethnic minorities. In the first two years of his administration, immigration to the United States soared to new records. With the outbreak of World War I in Europe, immigration fell away by record numbers.

During the Wilson years, public attitudes against immigrants hardened. As Wilson left office in 1921, Congress passed the most restrictive immigration law in American history and followed it in 1924 with more drastic restrictions.

The trip across stormy seas tested the newcomers' bravery and stamina. Their adjustment to the United States tested their souls. Each immigrant group faced pressure to conform to "American ways." This pressure came from families themselves and from forces outside the family. Israel Zangwill expressed this pressure to Americanize in his 1908 play, *The Melting Pot*, in which a Jewish immigrant abandons his old-world ways in order to embrace American values and "melt" into an American.

Many immigrants abandoned past attachments as they sought happiness in the New World. "Be a good American. This is a wonderful country for Jews," Louis Dershowitz told his grandson.

However, Americanization was a loss as well as a gain, a process that brought pain and anguish as well as joy. It was an exciting hope and exhilarating quest for success. But it required vast changes in family and ethnic values and a new perspective and identity.

Americanization began with learning the English language. Learning English was hard for adult immigrants, and some never mastered the language. But the immigrants' children attended American schools and learned English quickly.

A new, American-educated generation rejected "foreign"

Ethnic Newspapers

Back in 1914 the Massachusetts Commission on Immigration issued a report on the 58 foreign language newspapers published in the state in Albanian, Armenian, French, German, Greek, Italian, Lettish, Lithuanian, Polish, Portuguese, Swedish, Syrian, and Yiddish. The commission found the papers played a role in protecting public health, improving social, industrial, and political conditions, and in promoting schools, libraries, and lectures. It concluded:

> Six of these are dailies. In addition, many foreign-language papers published in other states have a wide circulation in Massachusetts. Although these papers find it very difficult to hold the second generation as readers, they are the only newspapers read by a large percent of the adult immigrant population.
>
> The policy and character of these papers differ widely. They represent the various religious and political factions of Europe as well as of the United States. All of them are, as to be expected, strongly "national" in the advocacy of the cause of their own people in the struggles of rival European races.... ■

words and accents, incorrect English grammar, and old-world gestures. Some children simply avoided bringing home classmates to meet parents whose English was weak. A knowledge of English was the passport to success for the young, but this difference in language became a wide gulf between immigrant parents and their children.

A tug of war raged in some families. "They make many sacrifices to keep their traditions," said a Jewish boy of his parents, "but they don't mean anything much in my life." His parents wanted him to take Hebrew lessons, but he wanted to play baseball and spend time with classmates who were not Jewish.

Even as parents argued, they agreed that success in America required learning English and making other adjustments. Mothers and fathers came to respect the agility their sons and daughters displayed in learning how to cope with "the land of opportunity." But parents also experienced a loss and sadness as their children embraced American materialism and pursued financial success.

In the Wilson years, white Protestant leaders increasingly began to express fear about immigrants. Could so many European

A Norwegian American Challenge

Ole Rolvaag, born in Norway in 1876, arrived in the U.S. at 20. He attended some Norwegian American schools in South Dakota and afterward St. Olaf College, in Northfield, Minnesota, where he remained as a teacher for the rest of his life.

Rolvaag studied his people's folklore and urged fellow Norwegian Americans to cherish their cultural background. The alternative, he explained, was to become "strangers to the people we forsook and strangers to the people we came to."

Assimilation, he believed, led to rootless individuals and an American civilization empty of beauty or substance. Ethnicity could make "a future rich in tradition and progressive in spirit."

In 1924 Rolvaag wrote *Giants in the Earth*, a novel about ethnic adaptation to America. Published in Oslo in 1924 and translated into English for a U.S. edition three years later, it has been called the best fictional account of the immigrant experience. ■

Catholics and Jews be absorbed easily, or at all? Some "old stock Americans" doubted that the newcomers would accept democracy or hard work and follow established Protestant traditions.

Increasingly, patriotic organizations and newspapers demanded that all immigrants learn English and "American ways." Those who held conservative or superpatriotic views, such as the Daughters of the American Revolution and the Sons of the American Revolution, insisted that newcomers also be taught "obedience to law... the groundwork of true citizenship."

As World War I approached, distrust of foreigners in America rose. Patriotic speakers voiced suspicion of immigrants with "divided loyalties." Some worried that various nationality groups might drag the country into a war to defend lands of their birth.

This alarm generated greater pressure for assimilation. Patriots said that public schools must drill immigrants in "the American way." Educators redefined the role of education. Schools were now supposed to demand political compliance from children born to foreigners and to make them into flag-waving, English-speaking U.S. citizens.

Some Americans had once voiced the hope that schools would teach each newcomer industrial skills, Americanization, and good citizenship. After that, they believed, patriotism would follow. But now many Americans feared foreigners in America. Both former President Roosevelt and President Wilson began to warn about "hyphenated-Americans." Of hyphenated-Americans, it was said, "only part of them came over here from the old country."

When Europe was plunged into war in 1914, this prejudice against foreigners became more intense. School classes promoted patriotism and political conformity. Newspapers talked of the many foreign "strangers" who might "stab [America] in the dark."

On July 4, 1915, "Americanization Day" was celebrated in 107 U.S. cities with the slogan, "Many Peoples, But One Nation." Soon after, the patriotic figures who arranged the event insisted that loyalty meant support for U.S. war preparedness. They spoke ominously of secret alien perils and wrote a new slogan — "America First." The superpatriots claimed foreign birth was the soil in which "moral treason" was bred.

Wilson's real dread, however, was not foreigners but Imperial Germany and the Central Powers, his potential enemies. It was hard to prove though that a distant nation could threaten America. It was easier to focus public attention on an internal foe, nearby neighbors who appeared to be different.

The President used his preparedness campaign to target those who opposed war and favored peace. He warned that people who were lukewarm about war preparedness or who opposed war with Germany were a real threat to America. He lumped them with the "hyphenated-Americans" that people had been warned about.

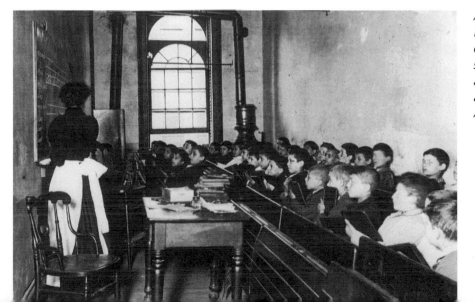

A school for immigrant children. U.S. schools taught assimilationism as well as Americanization.

*"Norwegian-
American" boy*

*"Swedish-
American" girl*

Business leaders in the National Association of Manufacturers and the U.S. Chamber of Commerce agreed with Wilson. Their real aim was to increase production and curb labor unrest, but association with the preparedness program wrapped them in patriotism. Employers ran English and citizenship classes for immigrants and stuffed patriotic literature into pay envelopes.

When the U.S. entered World War I in April 1917, Americanization shifted from a suggestion to a command. Wilson administration officials began a search for "disloyalty" and dissenters. Private groups such as the National Security League and the American Defense Society were given White House approval to saturate immigrant neighborhoods with prowar propaganda. Patriotic groups armed their members with prowar literature and sent them off to visit the foreign born.

As U.S. soldiers sailed for Europe in 1917, "Americanization" had become a part of the Wilson administration's effort to close down opposition to the war. The Justice Department compiled lists of people it called less than "100% American." In New York City, schoolchildren from immigrant communities were sent home carrying loyalty pledges for their parents to sign.

HOLLYWOOD

"The universal language has been found," said a man as he left a silent movie theater in the early 1900s. The movie camera was more than language, it was persuasion. Film images could reshape the nation for good or evil, and movies soon became a propaganda vehicle of enormous impact on American life.

Ethnic groups and women had been stereotyped in cartoons, novels, jokes, textbooks, and rhymes. But now these stereotypes leaped across screens to pound home their messages to huge audiences. From films the young learned to extol the virtues of "Americans" and to see some people as lesser and undeserving.

The American film industry developed during a time of rampant discrimination. Women did not vote, and men insisted that a woman's place was in the home. It was an age when Congress excluded Asians from these shores, citizens lynched people of color, and the public was being taught to fear immigrants from southern and eastern Europe. Movie screen stereotypes did not challenge but rather reflected America's most popular prejudices. It is ironic that the film industry which produced these stereotypes was run by immigrants who had themselves fled persecution in Europe.

By 1915, Hollywood's largest movie studios were owned by Jewish immigrants from eastern Europe. These businessmen or moguls decided who and what would appear in movies. The film industry was their dream come true since it made them rich.

Carl Laemmle, born in Laupheim, Germany, in 1867, began his American stay by first harvesting wheat in South Dakota and then by selling newspapers in Chicago. In 1906 he opened his first movie theater, the White Front. In 1912 he started Universal Studios and made it the top film distributor in the industry.

Other Jewish Americans followed his path. Adolph Zukor, born in Hungary, started Paramount Pictures. He introduced the idea that movies should run longer than an hour and exhibit more than a dazzling film technology. He wanted movies to tell important stories and to employ professional actors. Until his movie *Famous Plays and Famous Players* became reality, talented actors had ignored films.

Louis B. Mayer

William Fox, born in Hungary in 1879, turned a penny arcade he owned into a chain of 15 movie "palaces" and then started Twentieth Century Fox movie studio. Louis B. Mayer, born in Russia, arrived in Boston in 1904 without enough money for lunch, but came to own the huge film company Metro-Goldwyn-Mayer. Samuel Goldwyn, born in 1882 in Poland, landed in New York at age 11 and soon became a leading film producer. Four Warner brothers, Harry, Sam, Albert, and Jack, born to immigrants from Poland, left low-paying jobs in 1923 to launch the Warner Brothers company.

The movie moguls quickly rejected their Jewish heritage. "I'm an American not a Jew," said one. First the moguls Americanized their names. Samuel Goldwyn's real name had been Samuel Goldfish, and William Fox's real name had been Wilhelm Fried. Many movie moguls married Christian women at a time when only 2 percent of Jews married outside their religion.

As they found gold in the Hollywood hills, the moguls sought social acceptance through assimilation. They were fervently convinced that each immigrant wanted to (and should) assimilate and make money, and these beliefs found their way into their films.

Under their direction, Hollywood studios required leading male and female actors who could be identified with an ethnic group to take an "American" name. The scripts they approved for films also blared the clear message "be American." Since this approach reflected the viewpoint of most white Protestant Americans, the country's majority, it insured the popularity and profitability of the film studios.

The men who ran Hollywood also developed a knack for discovering and catering to American entertainment tastes and popular values. Films stressed loyalty to family, country, and the traditional leadership of America by Anglo-Saxons. The white Protestant bankers who financed Hollywood were pleased to support these ideas promoted by the movie studio owners.

In the film industry, the Hollywood moguls might have taken a different course and challenged stereotypes. They knew the death and pain persecution had brought to their families in Europe. However, they chose to distance themselves from that pain and to take a different, easier path.

Hollywood films promoted popular racist images, particularly when the camera was trained on people of color. In movies Native Americans were cast as evil, devious, vengeful "redskins." A few Indians were pictured as noble because they were loyal to whites, but even they were childlike and backward.

In a series of "greaser" films Mexican Americans were stereotyped as murderous villains. A few "greasers" proved they were good through their loyalty to Anglo Americans.

In 1922 the Mexican government officially complained to the U.S that such portrayals stirred "ill will toward Mexico" and soon banned films by companies producing the offensive caricatures. Then Spain, Panama, Nicaragua, and other Latin American nations signed treaties to end the importation of these derogatory films.

African Americans, victimized by society, were strung up again by Hollywood. D.W. Griffith's *Birth of a Nation* was the first film classic, the first American feature length film, and the first blockbuster. It also offered audiences a Ku Klux Klan version of American history and put its message across through innovative film techniques. *Birth of a Nation* turned Klan members into heroes. The film's villains were the former slaves who advanced democracy in the post-Civil War South.

When the film was shown at the White House, President Wilson called it "history written in lightning." For the first time a movie had a presidential stamp of approval. The next night Supreme Court Chief Justice Edward White was so thrilled at a showing that he proudly announced he rode with the Klan in Louisiana.

Actor Rudolph Valentino left Italy for the U.S. in 1913 at age 18. In 1921 he was Hollywood's first great "leading man."

Completed in 1913, the three-hour movie epic Birth of a Nation *depicted the Ku Klux Klan as heroes, while stereotyping Blacks. Protests and riots broke out in some cities where the movie was shown.*

African American groups protested *Birth of a Nation*'s distortion of history, particularly its effort to label leading black officials as rapists. Protests had it banned in 5 states and 19 cities. However, the picket lines and the scholarly refutations of the movie only increased its white audiences. Subsequently, black producers formed their own film companies to make movies that would more accurately reflect black life.

Hollywood's characterizations of Asians also reflected the hatred and laws that had banned Asian migration to the United States. Movie stereotypes rarely bothered to differentiate between Chinese and Japanese. If Asians and whites fell in love, tragedy resulted. Asian men were shown kidnapping white women and conspiring to conquer the world. In *The Yellow Menace* in 1916 Japanese and Mexican characters plot the military conquest of the United States.

Hollywood did more than degrade people of color. It omitted their part in American history. Westerns rarely included African Americans, Mexican Americans, or Chinese Americans as heroes, though many of these groups had helped build the West.

Pocahontas

In the 1908 movie *Pocahontas* whites were cast as Indians. *Variety* noted, "The Indians in *Pocahontas* looked like Chinese ballet girls must appear, if they have ballet girls in China."

Native Americans fought back. In 1911 a magazine reported two Chippewa delegations "had formed an uprising against moving pictures." The Chippewas planned to visit President William H. Taft and to ask Congress to regulate the content of films. They protested *Robby and the Redskin* in which a Native American high school graduate returns to his reservation, becomes an alcoholic and a criminal, and is tracked down and slain by white lawmen. ■

Before Jewish entrepreneurs took command of Hollywood, silent films had stereotyped Jews as conniving merchants and lawbreakers. In 1908 in *Levitsky's Insurance Policy*, a Jewish crook is cheated by an ordinary thief, to everyone's delight.

The new moguls of Hollywood, however, did produce a number of "ghetto films" that sympathetically illuminated the harsh conditions faced in sweatshops, particularly by young women. Other movies tried to depict Czarist pogroms against innocent Russian Jews. The Jewish American studio owners did permit the poorly coordinated Jewish soldier or cowboy to become a sympathetic film figure.

The "New Immigrants" from southern and eastern Europe received a mixed review in movies. In early cartoons, Italians were portrayed as swarthy, squat figures and sometimes as criminals. In later films they became gentle but emotional street vendors. In 1931, in *Little Caesar*, they were stereotyped as evil, deadly criminals who enjoyed the violence they created.

In Charlie Chaplin's *The Immigrant*, Europeans are shown reaching these shores pathetic and penniless. The comedian who made the voyage himself fondly portrayed the newcomers' courage, humor, and tenacity. Other films were less kind.

Often Hollywood stereotyped men from eastern and southern Europe as muscular, short, often crude and naive, and sometimes rigid and brutal. Immigrant women were usually dressed in black and pictured as sad, frightened, and submissive to men. They did not voice their own opinions or demonstrate any imagination. German American men, shown as fat from drinking beer and overeating, badly misused the English language.

British immigrant Charlie Chaplin became the greatest film comedian in the world.

But these film stereotypes were more comic than vicious. When some early films showed German immigrants as wild-eyed anarchists out to destroy capitalism and murder public officials, Hollywood was targeting radical political groups more than German Americans.

During World War I, Hollywood suddenly turned Germans into savage "Huns" who bayoneted children in Belgium, raped women in France, and tried to sabotage America's war effort. In *The Hun Within* in 1918, a German American becomes a secret agent for Germany and plants bombs on an American troop ship bound for France.

War movies such as *To Hell with the Kaiser* railed at Germany's rulers and questioned the loyalty of German Americans. Finally, in 1930 German soldiers in *All Quiet on the Western Front* were shown as human beings who laugh, starve, and fight on senselessly showing the futility of war.

EARLY 20TH CENTURY BLACK PROTEST

For African Americans, 90 percent of whom lived in the southern states as landless and voteless peasants, the years that led to World War I were unhappy ones. In 1913 educator Booker T. Washington, the leading African American figure of the day said, "I have never seen the colored people so discouraged and bitter as they are at the present time."

Booker T. Washington stands between President William H. Taft and inventor Andrew Carnegie.

Washington had long urged his people not to leave the South, or join unions, or agitate for equality. He urged them to pursue not a liberal education but "work with their hands" as farmers, blacksmiths, and cooks.

Washington's acceptance of segregation won him powerful white friends who provided funds for his educational programs. But his leadership was challenged by more militant African Americans. William Monroe Trotter of the Boston *Guardian* opposed "the Washington compromise," and journalist Ida B. Wells disputed Washington's right to surrender his people's fight for equality.

W.E.B. Du Bois, Harvard's first black Ph.D., became Booker T. Washington's most eloquent opponent, though the two men agreed on the need for racial solidarity and self-help. But Du Bois wanted to fight rather than accept the white racism that held his people down.

The struggle for equality faced an uphill battle. In the southern states African Americans lived under the threat of mob violence and lynchings. In the North, they faced silent barriers to their progress and occasional outbursts of violence. In Brownsville, Texas, three companies of African American soldiers of the 24th Infantry Regiment had a shoot out with local white bigots. President Teddy Roosevelt dishonorably discharged the three companies of these dedicated soldiers. Some senators called this a cruel, unjust decision based on racist thinking.

In 1907 whites in Atlanta, Georgia, rioted for three days against African Americans. Some Blacks armed to defend their homes, and others fled. No action was taken against the rioters, but an interracial Atlanta Civil League formed to aid race relations.

Then, in 1908, whites in Springfield, Illinois, Abraham Lincoln's home town, attacked local black residents. Hundreds of Blacks sought safety in the state militia barracks, and 200 fled the city.

The riot drew the attention of white journalist William English Walling and his Jewish immigrant wife, Ann Strunsky, who had once been jailed in Russia for her liberal views. In Springfield, the Wallings were shocked to find the white mob had been more ferocious than Russians in pogroms against Jews. White rioters they interviewed were not ashamed but proud of what they did. Walling wrote a magazine article that laid bare the violent racism in the North and then called on all citizens, in the spirit of Lincoln, to protect the rights and lives of African Americans.

Mary White Ovington agreed with Walling. As a reporter, she had researched black communities. Ovington and Walling then met with Henry Moskowitz, an assistant to the mayor of New York City and an expert on immigration. Publisher Oswald Garrison Villard, a grandson of William Lloyd Garrison, helped them draft a plan. On Lincoln's 100th birthday in 1909, 55 reformers and educators, whites and African Americans, called a conference on African Americans' constitutional rights.

W.E.B. Du Bois participated in the conference, as did Ida Wells, William Trotter, and clergymen Bishop Alexander Walters and Rev. Archibald Grimke. As a courtesy, Booker T. Washington was invited to the meeting, but, knowing that his strongest critics has organized it, he decided not to attend.

Out of this conference grew the National Association for the Advancement of Colored

W.E.B. Du Bois, author of 30 books, devoted his life to scholarship and civil rights.

Dr. Du Bois

William E.B. Du Bois, born in 1868 as his people gained the right to vote in the South, died the day before Dr. Martin Luther King gave his famous "I have a dream" speech in Washington, D.C., in 1963. To inform the world about the accomplishments of Africans and African Americans, he wrote 30 books including historical and sociological studies and novels.

Du Bois believed that a "talented tenth," an elite of educated African Americans like himself, had to lead the struggle for racial justice. In 1905 he and his followers organized a conference at Niagara Falls, Canada. They did not meet in the U.S. because hotel managers denied them rooms on the American side of the falls. By 1909, W.E.B. Du Bois' "Niagara movement" had laid the foundation for the NAACP.

Du Bois also began the pan-African movement in 1900, took part in the first World Races Conference in 1911, and organized a Pan-African Congress in Paris during the Versailles Peace Conference of 1919. He devoted his life to the fight for peace and equal justice around the globe and to educating people about the role African Americans played in American history. He took a leading part in efforts to free Africa from colonial rule and in campaigns against European imperialism in the world. Few men and women have had so great an impact on their times. ■

People (NAACP). Du Bois became the founding editor of its magazine, *The Crisis.* For the next decade, however, most NAACP officers were white women and men. Among its women officials were Lillian Wald, Jane Addams, Mary Ovington, Florence Kelly, and black educator Mary Church Terrell.

The first issue of The Crisis, *edited by Dr. Du Bois.*

Jewish Americans, such as Henry Moskowitz, Lillian Wald, and Joel and Arthur Spingarn, played a leading role in the early NAACP. They were also joined by Rabbi Stephen Wise, philanthropist Jacob Schiff, and attorneys Felix Frankfurter and Louis Marshall, president of the powerful American Jewish Committee.

Filled with determination and spirit but with few paid workers and little cash, the NAACP prepared to protect the legal rights of African Americans. Its first case was that of a young Black arrested for murder. Without evidence, he was charged with murder simply because he was found near the crime scene. He was put through the third degree by police and signed a confession, but an NAACP attorney won his release.

Following Ida Wells historic antilynching campaigns, the NAACP investigated and exposed these incidents. It also gave legal representation to people whose homes were dynamited or fire bombed because they moved into white neighborhoods.

NAACP attorneys brought antidiscrimination cases to the U.S. Supreme Court. Their first victory outlawed the grandfather clause in which southern states had denied African Americans voting rights because their grandfathers, as slaves, had not voted. Another NAACP victory came when the court outlawed legal agreements

The NAACP's Mr. White

In 1893, Walter White was born to light-skinned African American parents in Georgia. He grew up with blond hair, blue eyes, and a whitish complexion, but when he was 13 the Atlanta riot told him he was indeed a black man. He saw his father, rifle in hand, guard the family home against angry white rioters.

In 1918, White became an NAACP investigator. Using his "white" look as a disguise, he spent 10 years uncovering the facts about 41 lynchings and 8 race riots. He attended Ku Klux Klan meetings and heard lynchers talk about their crimes. Once he was sworn in as an Oklahoma deputy sheriff and told by a lawman that now he could "go out and kill all the niggers you can see and the law'll be behind you." On one occasion when lynchers found out White was an African American, he barely escaped with his life by hopping a train.

White bravely collected his evidence, including photographs of murderers at the scene of their crimes. Nevertheless, no convictions followed.

White also served for years as director of the NAACP. He often urged the U.S Congress to pass a federal antilynching law, but again nothing happened. He died in 1955. ∎

that prevented people from selling their homes to African Americans.

In *The Crisis*, Du Bois detailed racial crimes, published fiction and poetry by African Americans, and recounted tales of little known heroes of Africa and African America. He listed every black man or woman who graduated from college at the time or wrote a book. Du Bois' first editorial launched a drive against segregated schools with these words: "This is wrong and should be resisted by black men and white."

In the South NAACP membership or a subscription to *The Crisis* could lead to violence. In Mississippi, Rev. E.R. Franklin, who sold *The Crisis* subscriptions, was beaten by a mob, arrested the next day, and sentenced to 6 months on a chain gang. In 1918 John Shilliday, the NAACP's first executive director was beaten and kicked by a mob because he tried to bring antilynching petitions to the governor of Texas. Shilliday never fully recovered and was replaced by poet and author James Weldon Johnson, the NAACP's first African American director.

The NAACP also challenged the white media for featuring stories of black criminals and ignoring black accomplishments. Since this approach encouraged racial animosity and violence, NAACP official Joel Spingarn introduced the idea of annually awarding a gold medal to the outstanding African American. The "Spingarn Medal" was awarded to biologists, composers, authors, college presidents, poets, and civil rights crusaders. This also increased public awareness of African American achievements.

Dr. George Haynes

In 1911, another organization, the National Urban League, was started to help the large numbers of African Americans who left rural life for cities. Its earliest leaders included Frances Kellor and black scholars George Haynes and Eugene K. Jones who became its director. The league asked businesses and labor unions to cease practicing racial discrimination. In 1923 Charles S. Johnson began to publish the league's journal, *Opportunity*, which provided news about the organization and served as an outlet for young African American writers.

CHAPTER 4

BLACK MIGRATION

"We make just enough to keep in debt," reported an African American tenant farmer in Georgia early in the 19th century. In the South white supremacy denied people of color an education, job advancement, voting rights, and justice. A one party, one race white dictatorship ruled black lives. If African Americans fled their jobs, southern sheriffs arrested and returned them as though they were still slaves.

Under a "convict lease system," black men were convicted of minor crimes then rented out as laborers to local farmers. One victim told of working for the white man who paid his $50 fine.

> At the end of a month I find that I owe him more than I did when I went there. The debt is increased year in and year out....It is simply that he is charging you more for your board, lodging, and washing than they allow you for your work, and you can't help yourself either, nor can anyone else help you because you are still a prisoner and never get your fine worked out.

Another man found his life in rural Mississippi was a nightmare.

> In the South you had to work whether you wanted to or not.... Men and women had to work in the fields. A woman was not permitted to remain at home if she felt like it.... After the summer crops were in, any of the white people could send for any Negro woman to come and do the family washing at 74 cents to $1 a day.

Thousands of African Americans left rural areas for cities. Gradually, they became a majority in

This is a 1936 photograph of a plantation owner and his tenant farmers in Mississippi.

In 1927 African American policemen, such as this man in Harlem, New York City, began to appear on urban streets.

Charleston, Savannah, Baton Rouge, Vicksburg, Jacksonville, Montgomery, and Shreveport. Men became urban laborers, women domestics, nursemaids, and cooks. There was little chance for advancement, though a few men became foremen, and some women became better paid chefs.

As some people of color climbed into the middle class, in 1900 Booker T. Washington organized the National Negro Business League. By 1907, it had 320 branches and recruited hundreds of small entrepreneurs across the country.

In the South, African Americans often combined their resources to finance businesses in Atlanta, Hampton, Jacksonville, and Chattanooga. By 1914, 45 black banks, often affiliated with fraternal societies, had opened. Since they catered to a population without savings or capital, few survived for long.

Between 1910 and 1920 an estimated half a million African Americans left the rural South for jobs in the North. Many were driven by the boll weevil infestation that, by 1915, had wormed its way through the southern cotton crop. Then the next year severe floods struck the South, forcing more Blacks to leave.

The North offered powerful attractions for black workers who lived without hope for themselves or their children. "I want to come north where I can educate my three little children, also my wife," wrote a Mississippi lumber worker to a Chicago newspaper.

Black migrants at first left the rural South for Atlanta, Memphis, and Birmingham. Then as World War I dried up the stream of immigrants that industries had counted on for labor, they headed North.

The war produced a surge in factory orders and a demand for labor. People of both races were drawn northward by the hope of a good job, a decent home, education, and the glitter of city life.

A Chicago commission investigating working conditions found:

> Farmers and plantation workers coming to Chicago had to learn new tasks. Skilled craftsmen had to relearn their trades when they were thrown amid the highly specialized processes of northern industries.

The commission interviewed the African American newcomers and recorded these statements. "I make and save more money."

"Work is hard, but hours are short." "There are schools for the children, better wages." "More places to go, parks and playgrounds for children, and no difference made between white and colored." "We can live in good neighborhoods." "You can go where you want to go." "I can vote." "I can live without fear."

A black family that has arrived in Chicago from the South.

Some, however, complained about cold weather and crowded homes. Pointing to Chicago's many nightclubs and attractions, a woman warned about "not letting the life here run away with you." But in general people were very pleased with city jobs.

Chicago did not deliver on all its promises. Blacks could not join most unions or move into white neighborhoods. In a period of 3 years and 8 months, as some settled among whites, there were 58 racial bombings, one every 20 days. No one was jailed for these.

African Americans in Detroit also found good jobs, homes, and white animosity. In 1925 Dr. Ossian Sweet returned from France, where he had studied radium with Madame Curie, and bought a home in a white neighborhood. For 9 months before the Sweets moved in, they were threatened with death. Every night after they moved in, white crowds gathered in front of the Sweet home. The police stood by to prevent trouble but did not disperse the crowds. One evening a car filled with the Sweet's relatives arrived for a visit, and the whites charged after them. Dr. Sweet later testified in court about what happened next:

A black urban protest against "Jim Crow," or discrimination.

> When I opened the door and saw the mob, I realized that I was facing the same mob that had hounded my people through its entire history.... I knew what mobs had done to my race before.

As Dr. Sweet slammed the door on the mob, a shot rang out from an upstairs window, and a white man fell dead in the street.

The Birth of Jazz

Around 1900 African American bands combined a mixture of African, French, and Spanish melodies, beats, and instruments to create a music first called ragtime and then jazz. Its birthplace was New Orleans. Jazz used voodoo chants, West Indian tunes, French quadrilles, field songs, blues, and Christian hymns.

White New Orleans musicians crossed the color line to learn from jazz greats such as Joe "King" Oliver and Louis Armstrong. The Jack Laine white band included a Mexican American, Morton Abraham, two African Americans, Achille Baquet and Dave Perkins, Italian Americans George and Richard Brunies, and Johnny Stein, a Jewish American.

After World War I, New Orleans jazzmen moved to Chicago and New York and were joined by blues singers such as Ma Rainey and Bessie Smith. The new music was taken up by sons of European immigrants, such as Leon "Bix" Beiderbecke, descended from German immigrants. By the 1920s, American jazz had dazzled the young and become popular throughout the world. ■

Top: Ma Rainey's jazz band in 1924. Bottom: Leon "Bix" Beiderbecke.

Bessie Smith became the greatest blues singer of all time.

The police arrested every man and women in the Sweet house and charged these Blacks with various counts of murder.

To defend the Sweets, the NAACP hired Clarence Darrow, the most famous attorney of the day. The prosecution denied a mob had assembled that fateful night. Darrow pointed out the prosecution had "put on enough witnesses who said they were there to make a mob." The man slain that night, said Darrow, was not innocent since he had been part of a mob bent on violence. Darrow concluded by saying that African Americans also had a right to defend home and family. The jury agreed and found the Sweets not guilty.

CHAPTER 5

HARLEM: THE MAKING OF A CULTURAL MECCA

One major destination of the vast black migration was Harlem, a part of Manhattan in New York City. People of color had begun moving to Harlem after 1900 when rioting had shattered their neighborhoods in lower Manhattan. Harlem had once been a one horse town and then a center of fashion for the wealthy. It once had been home to white immigrants who had "made it" as bankers and businessmen, and polo was played in the Polo Grounds. Then white families began to leave Harlem, and it became African America's shimmering cultural center in America.

Thousands of African American families arrived to rent Harlem's sturdy, durable houses. In 1914 Harlem offered what the Urban League called "life in grand style, with elevator, telephone and hall boy service." By World War I, almost every major black church, YMCA, business and insurance company, settlement house, and civil rights organization had a home there. In 1920 Harlem had 80,000 residents and by 1930, 200,000. It held more Blacks than Birmingham, St. Louis, and Memphis combined.

Thousands of people from the Caribbean came to Harlem. By 1920, after hurricanes had destroyed many farms, about 50,000 West Indians sailed to America. By 1930, another 30,000 had entered the U.S. About 99 percent of these West Indians read English, and the men were largely skilled craft workers. In Harlem, where West Indians were 15 percent of the population, their British accents, Anglican church services, and loyalty to the British Crown made them distinctive individuals, and their calypso music blended with jazz, blues, and church hymns.

But West Indians came from a land where people of color had been a confident majority. In New York they reacted angrily to bigotry. Many refused to seek American citizenship. West Indians

Public School 89 in Harlem, New York City.

became known for an ability to band together and to save enough cash to start their own business ventures.

Harlem also attracted immigrants from Martinique, Haiti, and Guadeloupe who brought their own dances, songs, and wines — and their versions of the French language and the celebration of Bastille Day. Two African American researchers discovered 30 Caribbean ethnic clubs thriving in Harlem.

Black Spanish-speaking Puerto Ricans also left their island for Harlem. Between 1910 and 1930 the number of Puerto Ricans entering the U.S. mainland rose by more than 50,000, and many settled in East Harlem.

New York City had often served as a refuge for Puerto Rican *independistas* who sought to free their island from Spain: Ramon Emeterio Betances (1827-1898), who organized Puerto Rico's first attempt at a republic; independence fighter Eugenio Maria de Hostos (1839-1903); Francisco Gonzalo Marin (1863-1897), who published a revolutionary paper in New York; Santiago Iglesias (1872-1939), founder of the island's Socialist Party; and noted statesman Luis Muñoz Rivera (1859-1916).

After the island became an American possession, the exiles left for home. In 1917 Congress passed the Jones Act that granted Puerto Ricans who wished it U.S. citizenship. However, many islanders used their option to refuse American citizenship.

The Jones Act also stimulated migration, for Puerto Ricans

came to the United States not as foreigners but citizens. Health and educational conditions improved on the island under United States rule, but many young Puerto Ricans left the island for jobs and urban life in the mainland United States. After World War I, a Puerto Rican community formed near the Brooklyn Navy Yard in New York City. By 1930, East Harlem in Manhattan had become *El Barrio*, the neighborhood, the largest neighborhood of Puerto Rican Americans on the mainland United States.

In 1916 life in Harlem changed dramatically for African Americans when Marcus Garvey arrived from Jamaica to preach racial pride and to help his people save Africa from colonialism. Garvey formed the Universal Negro Improvement Association (UNIA) and preached "Africa for the Africans." Thousands of men and women marched in his parades. His paper, *Negro World*, in English, Spanish, and French, sold 200,000 copies weekly. No leader had touched black people as did this determined Jamaican prophet.

Marcus Garvey

From his Harlem offices, Garvey exhorted people to study their history, rejoice in their blackness, and build a sturdy motherland in Africa. He called whites "devils" and was critical of African Americans who had entered the middle class or who had light skins. He promised Africa's deliverance as agents of his Black Star Steamship Company sold stock across the country.

Garvey's flamboyant manner and utopian plans mobilized the poor but infuriated wealthy, educated, and successful Blacks. Some called him "the Jamaican Jackass." Civil rights figures were furious when Garvey met with a Ku Klux Klan leader, but criticism did not ruffle Garvey or his followers. He said that Klansmen, unlike other whites, were not hypocritical about their racism.

Garvey never visited Africa and spoke no African languages. But in 1920 he declared himself Provisional President of Africa and soon began an African Orthodox church, an African Legion, the Black Cross Nurses, a hotel, and a publishing company. He traveled to black ghettoes in 48 states with his message of "Up, you mighty people." He urged people of color to plan their own destiny.

J. Edgar Hoover of the U.S. Justice Department was alarmed by Garvey's ability to unite millions of African people. To Hoover, a person with Garvey's following was a threat to national security. Federal agents infiltrated the UNIA and other Garvey programs seeking evidence of criminal offenses, and in 1922 Garvey was indicted for mail fraud. The next year Garvey was tried before a white jury, convicted, and sentenced to 5 years in an Atlanta prison. In 1927 he was deported to Jamaica. Garvey died poor in London in 1940, but he was not forgotten. Dr. Du Bois, one of his many critics, praised Garvey's "tremendous vision, dynamic force, stubborn determination, and an unselfish desire to serve."

In the 1920s Harlem began a vast commemoration of African culture. Called the Harlem Renaissance, this movement was composed of poets, artists, and writers of color, young men and women who used their poetry, short stories, plays, and novels to capture the beauty of African American and African life. Their writings also became weapons to protest racism.

Claude McKay, a Jamaican author credited with initiating the Harlem Renaissance, wrote *Harlem Shadows* in 1922. He then wrote two famous novels, *Home to Harlem* (1928) and *Banjo* (1929). He is best remembered for his poem "If We Must Die," that promised black retaliation against lynch mobs.

Zora Neale Hurston, the leading woman writer of the Renaissance, was born in Florida in 1901 and wrote about her childhood home, the all-black town of Eatonville. She graduated from Morgan College and then Columbia University where she studied anthropology with Dr. Franz Boas, who led the scientific fight against racism.

Zora Neale Hurston

Impulsive and restless, Hurston worked with fellow authors, Langston Hughes (with whom she wrote the play, *Mule Bone*) and novelist Wallace Thurman. Her work took her back to Eatonville and to Louisiana where she studied voodoo rituals and wrote *Mules and Men*. In 1942 she wrote her autobiography, *Dust Tracks on a Road*, which became her most admired work.

Countee Cullen, born in New York City in 1903, won writing prizes at De Witt Clinton High School and at New York University. In 1925, he published *Color*, his best collection of verses. He taught in Harlem schools for 20 years and yet wrote a novel and nine other books of verse.

Countee Cullen

Langston Hughes, born in 1902 in Missouri, could trace his Indian ancestry back to Pocahontas, and his African ancestry to one of John Brown's raiders and a Virginia congressman. At his Kansas high school, young Hughes won a poetry contest but was denied the award because of his color. In his teens, Hughes began to write books. He came to New York in 1921 to enter Columbia University as a freshman, but he later explained he had come to New York "to see Harlem."

> I was in love with Harlem long before I got there, and I still am in love with it. Everybody seemed to make me welcome. The sheer dark size of Harlem intrigued me.

Langston Hughes signing autographs for some young admirers.

In 1926 his *Weary Blues* was published. Hughes visited France, Haiti, the Soviet Union, and Spain, but his experiences in Harlem had the most profound effect on him. His poetry, plays, newspaper columns, and autobiographies made him the poet laureate of urban America.

Arthur Schomburg

One of the most significant migrants to Harlem was Arthur Schomburg who arrived from Puerto Rico as a teen in 1891. Stirred by his ancestor's history in Africa and the New World, Schomburg had begun to collect books, pamphlets, and pictures by or about people of color.

In Harlem he opened his large library to the poets and writers of the Harlem Renaissance. During travels to Latin America, Europe, and throughout the United States, Arthur Schomburg continued to gather rare materials about Africans. In 1926 the Carnegie Foundation purchased his massive collection of 5,000 books, 3,000 manuscripts, 3,000 pamphlets, and 2,000 pictures and presented them to the New York Public Library. They became the basis for the famous Schomburg Center for Research in Black Culture, the largest single repository of such materials in the world. The Schomburg Center is located in Harlem. ■

CHAPTER 6

MEXICAN AMERICANS: ADJUSTMENT AND UNITY

Mexican American migration to the United States increased after 1900, and in the next three decades 700,000 Mexicans crossed the Rio Grande into the United States. Many were driven by the years of turmoil and violence of the Mexican Revolution that had begun in 1910 and lasted for ten years. Most arrived to take jobs at higher wages than they received in Mexico.

More than 40 percent of Mexican-born Americans who came to the United States settled in Texas and over 30 percent in California. Most had come to work on railroads, on farms, and in factories. They found hard work, a grim life, and a white justice system that took little interest in their needs.

In the Southwest from 1900 to 1930, Mexicans and Mexican Americans were hired for low-paying, unskilled, and semiskilled jobs. One in every five women and more than three of every ten men worked as farm laborers. Only 10 percent of the men and one woman in a hundred owned or managed farms. Most families were migratory laborers moving from one farm crop to another at harvest time. Many returned to Mexico during the off-seasons.

Mexican Americans held little political power in the United States, even in those parts of the Southwest where they were a majority of the population. Until World War I, no Mexican American had been hired as lawmen or elected to office.

Along the Rio Grande, Mexican American outlaws Aniceto Pizana and Luis de la Rosa commanded bands of two dozen men each. They were celebrated as heroes because they fought the Texas Rangers.

Some Mexican Americans began to leave the Southwest for work in cities. Some sought jobs in Detroit auto plants, Chicago and Gary steel and meat plants, and Pennsylvania and Ohio steel mills.

By the 1920s, Chicago's Chicano population had soared from 4,000 to 20,000. In 1930, 15 percent of all Americans born in Mexico lived in the eastern and northern states.

In their 20th century migration, almost half of Mexican American wives and teenage daughters took jobs in domestic and personal service. Others worked in food and other packaging plants. Only 5 percent held sales positions. These women earned less than their men and white women.

Mexican Americans found little upward mobility in the United States when white bosses and foremen denied them advancement over whites. Nevertheless, a middle class emerged in the service industries. Other Mexican Americans reached middle-class status as owners of small stores and restaurants, or as schoolteachers.

Government agencies, religious societies, and social service societies initiated training programs for Mexican Americans in English, advanced occupational skills, and American civics. But white employers often opposed these efforts, fearful they would promote labor discontent, protests, and strikes.

As migrant laborers, Mexican Americans found it hard to sink their roots into United States soil, sustain their community life, and use the services America had to offer. To support families, migrant laborers were continually moving to the next job.

In the 1920s, when federal laws drastically cut immigration from Europe and Asia, migration from Mexico reached new heights. By the early 1920s, more than half of all Mexican Americans, including those born in Mexico, lived in crowded *barrios*, or neighborhoods. Though many continued to return to Mexico, a degree of community stability led to the creation of strong self-help organizations. *La Alianza Hispano-Americana*, formed in 1894 in Tucson, Arizona, was the largest. In the early 20th century it spread to other states and claimed 20,000 members.

These societies often were named after Mexican heroes. Some were established by women or included both sexes, and others appealed either to working-class or to middle-class people. Generally, these fellowships provided lectures, legal services, emergency loans, medical or life insurance, and a vibrant social life. Some ran schools or libraries to promote their culture, and others battled segregation and discrimination in the United States.

La Orden de Hijos de America (Order of the Sons of America), begun in 1920 in San Antonio, was made up of Mexican American white-collar workers determined to win full American citizenship rights.

Mexican American families found their Catholicism crucial to their survival. In their Catholic churches they melded Native American and Catholic rituals even when this led to disputes with their American clergymen. However, when Protestant missionaries tried to recruit Mexican Americans, they had little success.

Mexican Americans complained that the leaders of the church in the Vatican in Rome had failed to send enough priests to the southwestern United States and even fewer who could speak Spanish. By 1930, Catholic bishops in America had heard their pleas and had launched major campaigns to assist them.

Since they were denied membership in the American Federation of Labor and most other unions, employers often tried to use Mexican Americans to drive down white wage scales or to replace striking workers. Most Mexicans who crossed the Rio Grande, however, took jobs whites did not want.

Early in the 20th century, Mexican Americans organized their own strikes. In 1903 in the copper mines of Arizona, they struck to avoid a pay cut. Their effort ended when whites refused to join their strike and their Mexican American leaders were arrested.

In 1913 Mexican Americans struck to gain higher wages and better conditions in California. When they protested against the degrading conditions of farm labor in Wheatland, California, National Guard troops arrested 100 strikers. The strong effort of Mexican American workers did bring inhuman labor conditions to public attention and led to the creation of the California Commission on Immigration and Housing.

In 1915, 5,000 Mexican Americans in three local Arizona unions struck to end a dual-wage system that favored whites. This time whites came to their support, and they won equal pay. In 1917 and 1918, after the U.S. entered World War I, Mexican American strikes in Arizona copper mines were met by massive vigilante attacks.

The 1920s increase in immigrants from Mexico also produced new labor organizations in California. Mexican American grape-pickers in 1922 formed a union in Fresno. The Confederation of Mexican Labor Unions (CFLU) began in 1927, and its aim was to win equal pay and end discrimination. Its first strike, in the Imperial Valley in 1928, ended when state officials ordered the arrest of dozens of strikers. Two years later strikers in the Imperial Valley won their strike against their employers.

But growers reorganized, renewed their attack, and a few months later more than 100 laborers had been arrested. At its height the CFLU had 20 locals and 3,000 members.

While some fought for their rights as laborers, other Mexican Americans began to enter the democratic process. In 1915 Benigno Hernandez was elected to Congress from New Mexico. Two years later Ezequiel De Baca was elected the state's governor. In 1921, Nestor Montoya was elected to Congress from New Mexico. However, most Mexican Americans in the region remained poor and unaffected by these political gains.

Mexican Muralists in America

In 1927 Americans heartily welcomed the great Mexican artist José Orozco to New York for an opening at the Harriman Gallery of his *Drawings of the Revolution*. Orozco remained in the United States for nine years and completed murals for three colleges: Pomona College, in Claremont, California, The New School in New York City, and Dartmouth College in Hanover, New Hampshire. His work depicts Mexican historical themes.

In 1931 the Museum of Modern Art invited another great Mexican muralist, Diego Rivera, to New York when his works were presented. He stayed on to paint frescoes in Rockefeller Center, New York, San Francisco, and Detroit. Some of the powerful murals of Rivera and Orozco, because of their strongly pro-labor viewpoint, were later censored or removed by the sponsoring officials. ■

José Orozco

Diego Rivera

CHAPTER 7

WORLD WAR I

In 1914 World War I erupted in Europe as the Central Powers (Germany, Austria-Hungary, and Turkey) clashed with the Allies (Serbia, France, Russia, and England). More than 4,660,000 people, a third of all foreigners in the United States, had been born in Central Powers land but now saw themselves as Americans. Their labor aided the country's war effort, and their sons served in the American Expeditionary Force (AEF) in Europe.

Government officials and some prominent citizens began to focus public fears on those immigrants who came from lands controlled by the Central Powers. Innocent people were accused of being disloyal to the United States.

American opinion, rather than supporting either the Allies or the Central Powers, overwhelmingly favored a government policy of neutrality. A few Americans of British or French descent rushed off to volunteer with the Allied Armies. German Americans were proud of Germany's culture and sudden rise to world power but had no desire to fight for their former homeland. American Finns and Swedes were pro-Germany because Czarist Russia posed a threat to their homelands. Irish Americans and German Americans did not want to see England victorious and spoke out for neutrality. Greek Americans were divided between royalists who favored Germany and antiroyalists who opposed it. On the whole very few immigrants or other Americans wanted war.

World War I recruitment poster.

The Wilson administration secretly began to tilt toward the Allies before the 1916 election. The President risked war when he sent supplies to England, sometimes on passenger ships, through an Atlantic Ocean patrolled by German submarines. When ships were sunk and American lives were lost, Wilson called Germany a nation of fiends who killed innocent tourists at sea.

In 1916 Wilson was reelected on the slogan, "He kept us out of war." When he asked for a declaration of war against the Central

Powers in April 1917, he knew that most Americans still favored neutrality. To counter the peace sentiment, Wilson decided to whip up public support for the war to a "white heat." His Committee on Public Information (CPI) flooded the nation with prowar, anti-German, and pro-Ally propaganda.

The administration's propaganda offensive also tried to label those who opposed the war as disloyal. At Wilson's request Congress passed two "espionage laws" to punish "disloyal... or abusive words" about U.S. officials, uniforms, the flag, the Constitution, or the war. Serious opponents of the war were to be treated as dangerous criminals, prosecuted, and jailed.

Like native-born Americans, foreigners were pressured to demonstrate their loyalty, to buy Liberty bonds, and to enlist in the U.S. armed forces. Every foreigner, said one patriot, "must grow an American soul inside of him or get out of the country." These tensions began to divide patriotic immigrant families who also sought to preserve their ancient cultures.

Many foreign-born Americans faced persecution. Because Holland remained neutral during the war, arsonists in Iowa burned a Dutch school. Iowa officials changed Dutch street names. To prove their loyalty, Dutch Americans had to conduct their church services in English, give their children American names, and stop speaking Dutch in public.

This victory loan poster celebrates a multicultural America.

The war increased demands for "Americanization." Henry Ford hired foreigners but made them attend English classes in his factories. The first sentence each immigrant at Ford learned was "I am a good American." Immigrants then took part in a drama. They lined up, marched carrying foreign flags, climbed into a "melting pot," and emerged waving American flags.

About 18 percent of the foreigners in the United States (including German Americans) served in the U.S. armed forces, a higher percentage than the rest of the population. But in spite of this the United States government still kept alarm over alien disloyalty at a fever pitch.

The Wilson administration used this war hysteria to smash the Industrial Workers of the World (IWW), a union that had opened its doors to workers of both sexes and of all colors, religions, and nationalities. But the IWW also called strikes and had harsh words for capitalism and government, so the President decided its leaders were "German agents." Federal agents spied on IWW members, raided their meetings, arrested, and brought to trial hundreds of IWW leaders.

The war created a climate of fear that destroyed freedom of expression in many ethnic communities and made a mockery of democracy. Some speakers urged the banning of books and the ending of foreign language instruction in schools. South Dakota banned German and so did 200 other U.S. school districts. Some 25 state school systems actually banned the teaching of German. Minneapolis public schools banned 30 books. By May 1918, more than half of the state's high schools had blacklisted books, 93 had discarded books, and in 23 high schools censors had ripped out certain pages that were considered unpatriotic.

War animosity became so intense that it replaced other hatreds. Earlier racists had celebrated Germany's Teutonic "superiority." But after 1917, these bigots began to link Germans not with Teutonic heroes but with Asians and others collectively referred to as "the barbarian races."

The war brought new demands for conformity. Swedish-born Minnesota governor John Lind declared, "This is a just and holy war" and urged young men to enlist in the American army as "protectors of humanity." Swedish Americans in Illinois and Minnesota were arrested for refusing to register for the draft. The Minnesota Commission of Public Safety investigated Swedish Americans who showed an interest in socialism. Danish Americans and Norwegian Americans were divided over the war. But both ethnic groups were investigated for disloyalty.

Once war was declared, the many ethnic minorities swung into line. They joined the armed forces, helped the Red Cross, and aided the war effort in many different ways.

The sons and grandsons of immigrants accepted the draft. Thousands of Armenian Americans volunteered for a "Yankee" division recruited in Massachusetts. Private Vartan Aghababian of the 146th Infantry

A Red Cross photograph celebrates "Americans All." These are U.S. soldiers in France.

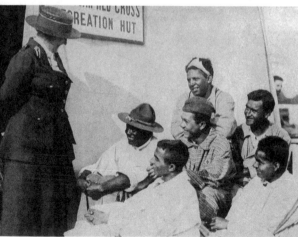

Regiment, wounded many times, became the first Armenian American awarded the Medal of Honor.

Some 215,000 Polish Americans joined the U.S. armed forces. The war stimulated their increased political role. Milwaukee elected its first Polish American congressman, Republican John Kleczka.

Some 6,000 Native Americans volunteered for the army. Their display of loyalty and battlefield courage helped persuade Congress in 1924 to granted citizenship to all Native Americans.

Latvian Americans joined the U.S. Army and Navy, and a Latvian War Association in Boston sold Liberty bonds and urged independence of Latvia. In 1918, 56 Latvian Americans in Boston took part in a patriotic parade under their own banner, for the first time marching as an identifiable group. However, Boston's Latvian American socialists held antiwar demonstrations.

Some 60,000 Greek Americans joined the armed forces, and their communities raised $30,000,000 in Liberty bonds. George Dilboy, a Greek American, earned the Medal of Honor only to lose his life while fighting in the Battle of Belleau Wood, France.

About 14,000 Arab Americans served in the U.S. armed forces. In 1919 a noted Arab scholar in the U.S., Abraham Mitrie Rihbany, was inspired to write a booklet, *America, Save the Middle East*. Over 15,000 Portuguese Americans served in the armed forces, including one of the first to die in combat, Private Walter Goulart.

American Czechs enlisted in the Canadian Army in 1916, and 3,000 American Czechs and Slovaks later joined Czechoslovak legions in France. Some 40,000 Czech and Slovak Americans fought as U.S. troops. Their relatives at home bought many Liberty bonds.

Czech Immigrant Emanuel Voska and his daughter, Villa, left Queens, New York, for Europe where he stole secret documents for British intelligence. Voska and a network of women operated behind enemy lines, and 80 of his agents infiltrated German and Austro-Hungarian embassies and shipping lines.

Romanian Americans, including 127 from Youngstown, Ohio steel mills, flocked to the armed forces. Some proudly asked to serve in the U.S. Army's Romanian Volunteer Legion.

Though Japanese Americans were rarely welcomed into the armed forces, they formed an American Loyalty League in San Francisco. Hidemitsu Toyota, an *Issei* who served the U.S. war effort, was rewarded with his naturalization certificate in 1921.

America's Jews, only 3.27 percent of the population, became 5.73 percent of the U.S. armed forces. The 9,177 Jewish American officers included an army general, a marine general, and a navy admiral. Three Jewish Americans won Congressional Medals of Honor, and 147 others earned Distinguished Service Crosses. Irish Americans, Italian Americans, and other ethnic groups also served in all three branches of the armed forces.

War fever often targeted German Americans. In 1918 one was lynched in Illinois for "making disloyal remarks." Some people in Minnesota the next month tarred and feathered a clergyman who prayed in German over a dying woman. Bruno Walter, noted conductor of the Chicago Symphony Orchestra, was fired because he was a German immigrant who had not become a U.S. citizen.

German names on city streets were changed. German music was shunned. Even hamburgers were renamed "Salisbury steaks," and sauerkraut became "Liberty cabbage." Few Americans learned that General John J. Pershing, who commanded the American army overseas, had a great-grandfather who emigrated from Germany.

German American social organizations and newspapers began to collapse under the strain of public hostility. Then, in 1919 German Americans organized a patriotic Steuben Society to Americanize remnants of Germany's past still alive in U.S. citizens. In reaction to the hatred coming from the Wilson administration, most German Americans became Republican voters. Ironically, in France, Pennsylvania's 28th U.S. Infantry Division, which included many German Americans, was one of the first American units to face combat against Germany's armies.

For many African Americans World War I posed the dilemma of fighting for democracy in Europe while being denied it at

African American "Silent Parade" in 1917 to protest lynchings and race riots.

home. Some 38 African Americans were lynched in 1917, the year the United States entered the war. As U.S. troops left for the battlefields of France in July, a white riot in East St. Louis took dozens of black lives. The NAACP led 15,000 marchers who protested the riot and lynchings with a "Silent Parade" down New York's Fifth Avenue. A month later whites in Houston, Texas, clashed with members of the black 24th Infantry Regiment, and 19 people lost their lives.

At first recruiting stations refused to enroll African American volunteers. Finally, some 700,000 registered under the Selective Service Act, and 367,000 were drafted.

Half of all the African Americans in the military served in the 92nd and 93rd Combat Divisions. The U.S. Army handed them over to French command and issued orders they were not to be allowed to mix with French civilians. But black troops became the first U.S. soldiers in battle, and entire African American regiments earned French medals for heroism. In May 1918, the 369th U.S. Infantry (15th New York Regiment) defended one-fifth of all territory held

Victorious African American soldiers return from the war front to the U.S.

Black U.S. troops in trenches in France.

by U.S. troops. It bore the brunt of Germany's July offensive and went on to become the first American Expeditionary Force to reach the Rhine River. It never lost an inch of ground or had a single man captured. Two members were the first U.S. soldiers to earn the French *Croix de Guerre*.

On the home front people of color purchased a quarter of a million dollars in Liberty bonds. In 1918, the year the war ended, however, 58 African Americans were lynched. Still a new breed of African American fighting man, who had fought for democracy in Europe, returned to the United States after the war.

Eugene Debs

Born in 1856 to Alsatian immigrants in Indiana, Eugene Debs became a prominent American labor leader. In 1900 Debs became the first presidential candidate of the new Socialist Party and won 100,000 votes. In 1908 he won 420,000 votes, and in 1912 the number increased to 900,000 votes.

Debs urged unity among all workers — foreign- and native-born, men and women, whites, immigrants, and people of color. "Every worker is your friend, and every boss is your enemy," was Eugene Debs' creed.

Debs called World War I an imperialist war and was arrested for making a speech against the draft. He refused to defend himself and instead used the courtroom to attack U.S. participation in the war and capitalism. Sentenced to 10 years in prison, Debs told the judge:

Your honor, years ago I recognized my kinship with all living things, and I made up my mind that I was not one bit better than the meanest on earth. I said then, I say now, that while there is a lower class, I am in it; while there is a criminal element I am of it; while there is a soul in prison, I am not a free man.

In 1920, from Atlanta Prison, Debs ran for president again and polled 920,000 votes. He was pardoned the next year, but jail had ruined his health, and he died in 1926. ■

A. Philip Randolph

Asa Philip Randolph was born in 1889 in Florida to the family of an African American clergyman. Young Randolph helped build railroads, and he sold newspapers and ran a delivery wagon. After he graduated from high school, he left for New York and enrolled in City College. Randolph worked as a porter, but he also studied economics and became a familiar political voice heard on Harlem street corners. In 1917 he began a newspaper, *The Messenger,* that denounced racism and called World War I white Europe's fight for colonies. Twice *The Messenger's* offices were invaded by government agents, seeking proof that Randolph was a German agent or a dangerous subversive.

For making an antiwar speech, Randolph was arrested and jailed. But upon his release, he continued to attack America's role in the war. Federal agents listed him as "the most dangerous Negro in America." It was a title he wore with pride.

In the 1920s Randolph organized the Pullman railroad car porters into the first strong African American union in the United States. Randolph went on to become the leading voice for racial equality in the labor movement for many decades. ■

Voices for Peace

President Wilson asked the United States Congress for a Declaration of War in April 1917. However, Congress was not unanimous in its support of the president.

Prominent U.S. women were part of the Ford Peace Mission before World War I.

A decade before war loomed in Europe, middle-class white women had formed dozens of pacifist groups. One pacifist leader was Mary Anderson, a Swedish immigrant who started in America as a maid. In 1915 Carrie Chapman Catt and Jane Addams formed the Women's Peace Party. Helen Keller had denounced militarism and war for decades.

In 1917 the Wilson administration jailed three people who opposed America's participation in World War I. ■

CHAPTER 8

WOMEN GAIN THE VOTE

As World War I approached, the struggle for women's suffrage gained steam. In 1890 the National American Woman Suffrage Association (NAWSA) was formed and led by Carrie Chapman Catt. In an age where there was fear of immigrants and people of color, NAWSA surrendered to these popular hatreds. Her suggestion was to "cut off the vote of the slums, and give it to women." Catt also asked for the suffrage for white women as "a means of legally preserving white supremacy in the South."

The NAWSA campaign for suffrage relied on massive parades and other protests. Some men and women complained this approach was "unladylike," but it worked. After their second parade in New York City, the *World* reported: "The ladies are.... demanding the vote and the scalps of their enemy."

In the election of 1912 Teddy Roosevelt ran for president not as a Republican but as a Progressive. Roosevelt agreed to support the women's suffrage amendment to the Constitution.

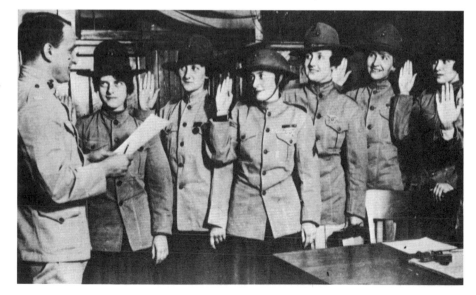

In August 1918, these women were sworn into the U. S. Marines.

Suffragist Alice Paul organized a march of 5,000 women in 1913 the day before Woodrow Wilson was inaugurated as president. Marchers were denied police protection and had to push their way through angry crowds. The women, reported a paper, "for the most part, kept their tempers."

The suffrage campaign accelerated after war broke out in Europe. Women left their homes for war jobs. They sold war bonds, made bandages, and worked for the YMCA and Red Cross. Some served overseas in European war zones. Suffragists pointed out it was hypocritical to claim women were unfit to vote.

After America declared war, President Wilson appealed to women for help, and more than a million replaced men who had to leave their jobs for the war front. Women made guns and bombs and built ships and tanks. Some Polish and Swedish American women in Pennsylvania repaired Erie railroad cars. "They move great wheels as if possessed of the strength of Hercules," wrote reporter Harriet Blatch. In the locomotive shops she "found women working on drill press machines with ease and skill."

Despite these efforts, women earned less than men doing the same job and were rarely promoted to supervisory positions. African American women were often denied war jobs, and when they were hired, they were segregated, given less pay, and denied promotions. Mary Church Terrell held a master's degree and could speak and write in German, Italian, and French. After her interview for a federal job, she was not called back or hired.

Mary Church Terrell fought for civil rights for most of her long life.

Adah Thomas fought for and won the right of African American women to serve as army nurses. She became one of three black women to serve American troops in France. She and Kathryn Johnson wrote of their exciting adventures at the war front in *Two Colored Women with the American Expeditionary Forces.*

The Wilson administration asked the suffrage movement to put aside their drive to gain the vote until the war was over. Instead, women said that a country in a war "to make the world safe for democracy" should grant them voting rights. Alice Paul and other suffrage leaders were often arrested for picketing the White House, and some were mistreated in prison.

Finally, in 1918 President Wilson announced his support for a suffrage amendment to the Constitution. The proposed 19th

Women on the Cutting Edge

Some women believed in a greater degree of activism than merely seeking the vote. Mary Harris was one of these women. Born in Cork, Ireland, in 1830 shortly before her family migrated to Toronto, Canada, young Mary Harris entered the United States and soon married a member of the Iron Holder's Union named Jones. Then, in 1867 a yellow fever epidemic killed her husband and four children.

Mother Jones

Jones began a dressmaking business in Chicago, but it was destroyed in the Chicago Fire of 1871. In her forties she became a labor agitator and was called "Mother Jones." Workers, she told audiences, must organize to match the power of their employers.

Businessmen often blamed "Mother Jones" for labor unrest, but to striking families she was their hero and a familiar visitor on their picket lines. In Alabama, she battled against textile mill owners who hired children of 4 to 7 years to work 8-hour shifts at 10 cents a day. She told audiences how tedious work, often close to hazardous machinery, led to accidents and deaths among children. But she also knew that parents, desperate because of their poverty, had to send their children to work. Jones denounced an economic system that pushed families into this type of decision.

Mother Jones often landed in jail for her participation in the miners' strikes. But still feisty and unbowed at 80, she told striking miners:

I don't care how much martial law the governor of West Virginia proclaims. I have had martial law proclaimed in other states where I have worked more than once and I did not stop fighting. When they took the martial law off, I began at once and he [the governor] had to bring the troops back.

Mother Jones often focused on organizing women or lifting the morale of strikers' wives. During a coal strike, she armed miners' wives with brooms and mops. Her "mothers' militia," some with infants in their arms, guarded mine entrances and turned back scabs. Mother Jones, who lived to be 100, died in 1930.

Helen Keller was born in Alabama in 1880. She was stricken with an illness that left her deaf, blind, and mute when she was two years old. Through Anne Sullivan, her dedicated teacher, Keller was able to learn to read Braille. She studied Greek, Latin, German, and French, graduated from Radcliffe College, and went on to become a voice for human rights all over the world.

Keller devoted her energy to aiding the victims of society—workers, minorities, women, and children. She also fought bigotry because it divided humanity. Her insights and dynamic delivery held audiences spellbound. Mark Twain called her "the greatest woman since Joan of Arc." In 1903 she wrote *The Story of My Life*, the first of 4 books.

Keller urged women to use hunger strikes to gain the vote.

They cannot hope to get anything unless they are willing to fight and suffer for it. The pangs of hunger during the hunger strike are a sample of the suffering they must expect.

Helen Keller

Keller saw capitalism and war as twin evils. "The burden of war always falls heaviest on the toilers," she said. "They are taught that their masters can do no wrong, and go out in vast numbers to be killed on the battlefield." Of war, she said:

Nothing is to be gained by the workers from war. They suffer all the miseries, while the rulers reap the rewards. Their wages are not increased, nor their toil made lighter, nor their homes made more comfortable. The army they are supposed to raise can be used to break strikes as well as defend the people.

Margaret Higgins, born in 1883, was one of 11 children of poor Irish immigrants. She was able to attend college because two of her sisters supported her. She married William Sanger in 1902 and the next year gave birth to the first of their 3 children. After 8 years as a bored wife, she took a job as a visiting nurse in New York's Lower East Side. The experience changed her life.

Sanger met immigrant women surrounded by babies they had not planned for. She decided that poor women were being crushed by society and their husbands, and her job was to rescue them.

In 1913 Sanger began a campaign to teach women about birth control. At that time most men and women would not discuss the issue. One of her first articles was censored by the United States Post Office, but the censorship helped publicize her crusade.

In 1914 Sanger fled to Europe after being indicted for publishing an article about birth control. She returned and began to recruit doctors and scholars for her campaign.

In 1921 Sanger launched the American Birth Control League, which in 1942 became Planned Parenthood. During the 1920s, largely as a result of her efforts, some states legalized birth control devices, but women still had to request them from doctors.

Sanger toured Europe, Asia, and Africa to teach women about birth control. By the time of her death in 1966, her daring and persistence had lifted a veil of shame that had clouded a vital human issue.

Margaret Sanger is thought of as a pioneer builder of health clinics for women, but her great gift to the world was a change in attitudes. She made it possible for women to openly discuss and seek medical aid for a basic aspect of their health. ∎

*Suffragettes
proudly
demonstrated for
the right to vote.*

Amendment passed the House of Representatives with the required two-thirds vote (274 to 136) and went on to the Senate. "We have made partners of the women in this war," said the president, as he urged the Senate to pass the amendment, but the Senate took two more years to approve the suffrage amendment.

To become part of the Constitution, a proposed amendment must be approved by three-quarters of the states. In January 1920 this requirement was met, and women's suffrage became the law of the land when the Tennessee legislature ratified the amendment. The deciding vote was cast by a 24-year-old man whose mother had ordered him to support it.

Actual eligibility to vote is determined by state governments. By the time the amendment was ratified, the western states and the New England states had already granted equal suffrage, and most others had passed partial women's suffrage laws. Only eight southern states did not grant some form of women's suffrage.

First proposed in 1848 at the Seneca Falls, New York, convention, passage of the 19th Amendment had taken nearly three-quarters of a century. More than 800 campaigns directed at state legislatures, political parties, and 19 successive Congresses had been waged by the suffrage movement since 1848.

*U. S. women
march to gain
suffrage.*

CHAPTER 9

POSTWAR PROBLEMS

In 1917, when Lenin's Communist Party seized control and established a Soviet government in Russia, U.S. war propaganda added this new target to anti-German hysteria. Fear of communism spread among industrialists, bankers, and many others all over the world.

A "Red Scare" fed by government officials and newspapers gripped the public. Any American who voiced "radical" or "foreign" ideas could be accused of being a Communist. Hatred toward "foreigners" did not end with World War I but increased in intensity and violence.

To prove their patriotism and "100% Americanism" citizens had to denounce "Red" Russia and "foreign ideas." In 1919 when more than 4 million steelworkers, coal miners, and other laborers went on strike, the public was told that Communists were at fault. When women cut an independent path for themselves, wore short skirts, asked for liberal divorce laws, or danced to jazz music, "Reds" were blamed. A popular magazine charged in rhyme that women's peace groups had fallen under Soviet control:

> Miss Bolsheviki has come to town
> With a Russian cap and a German gown.
> In women's clubs she's sure to be found,
> For she's come to disarm America.

White rioters attacked African Americans in Chicago and 24 other cities in 1919.

Many Americans became convinced the nation was in danger. In small towns in Iowa, Kansas, Oregon, and other states citizens began to fear they might wake up to find ruthless, foreign, bearded Communists marching down their main streets.

Blacks found the old bigotry was still intact after the war. In 1919, 76 African Americans were lynched, some still in their U.S. Army uniforms. Whites rioted against African Americans in 25 cities

across the country. This time, however, black neighborhoods in Chicago and Washington, D.C., armed themselves and fought back. To some whites this proved that "Reds" were at work.

Under the guise of combatting Reds, federal officials smashed nationwide steel and coal strikes and other efforts by labor to raise wages, reduce hours, or increase their benefits. Using the hysteria over communism and foreigners, Attorney General A. Mitchell Palmer, ordered a roundup of thousands of Russian aliens. In November 1919 his agents swooped down in dozens of cities to arrest members of the Union of Russian Workers (URW). A few of the arrested were probably Communists, but most were ordinary immigrants trying to learn English and American ways. However, thousands were beaten and jailed in the raids.

Justice Department officials deported 249 of the arrested aliens, including anarchist Emma Goldman, to Soviet Russia. Four were charged with anarchism, 47 "did not respect the government," and the others were simply URW members charged with no crimes. None had faced any accusers, heard any evidence, or received a trial. And being a Communist or an anarchist were not crimes. But Palmer claimed his agents had discovered guns, ammunition, "bomb factories," and "conspiracies to sabotage the government." And, he claimed, he had just begun to uncover subversive plots.

In January 1920, the attorney general launched new raids in three dozen cities. Only 3,000 warrants were issued, but Palmer and his assistant, J. Edgar Hoover, had their agents arrest 6,000 men and women. Hoover refused to permit those jailed to meet with lawyers. Bail was set at $10,000 (not the usual $500), and the imprisoned were not allowed to speak even to family members.

Palmer publicly announced that he had "halted the advance of 'red radicalism' in the United States." But only 550 of the 6,000 arrested aliens were found legally deportable.

Men and women had been kept in cells without sufficient food or water, and a few had been beaten until they confessed to crimes they did not commit. It was not foreigners but Palmer's denial of legal protection for his victims that threatened the Constitution.

Next Palmer announced he was a candidate for president. He predicted that Communists in America would revolt on May Day 1920, and that he and Hoover would be ready for their bombings and assassinations. May Day came and went peacefully, and so did Palmer's White House hopes. Citizens began to denounce Palmer's illegal measures, and the Justice Department had to release the thousands it had jailed.

But the war hysteria and the postwar Red Scare had fueled a rising intolerance against foreigners. In 1915 a Jewish American factory owner in Atlanta, Leo Frank, falsely accused of murder, was seized by a mob and lynched. This violence stimulated the birth of a new Ku Klux Klan the next year in Georgia. The Klan fed on the wartime hatred of Germans and other foreigners.

After the war, the new Klan broadened its hate program to focus on "mongrel civilization" — people of color, Catholics, Jews, ethnic minorities, and foreigners. It declared itself 100 percent American and opposed unions, independent women, and liberals. The Klan leader, Imperial Wizard William Simmons, warned of a deadly peril to America from

In 1925, 40,000 Klansmen marched in Washington, D.C.

...the tremendous influx of foreign immigration, tutored in alien dogmas and alien creeds, flowing in from all climes, and slowly pushing the native-born white American population into the center of the country, there to be ultimately overwhelmed and smothered.

The Klan claimed branches in 48 states and a membership of four million. It helped elect governors in Oklahoma, Oregon, and Indiana and put many officials into local offices. The Klan also claimed support from 100 congressmen and from presidents Warren G. Harding and Calvin Coolidge.

The Ku Klux Klan was one of many organizations demanding that Congress restrict migration, and in 1921 Congress passed an immigration act reflecting the national bias against people from eastern and southern Europe and Asia. Rigid quotas for different nations were written into this law. Admission to the United States was based on only 3 percent of those from each nation who lived here in 1910. This dramatically cut the "new immigration" from eastern and southern Europe which had comprised four-fifths of arrivals after 1910. Asians were further excluded, and the new quota law slashed immigration from Africa and other parts of the world. Immigration fell by one-half in one year as the new law kept out those most likely to come. However, people from England and northern Europe, here in large numbers before 1910, were automatically granted large quotas. These quotas often remained unfilled.

In 1924 Congress slashed immigration even further. It brought down the nationality quotas by another third, from 3 percent to 2 percent. The new law also moved the base year back 20 years from 1910 to 1890 when even fewer eastern and southern Europeans lived here than in 1910. This change automatically meant further sharp cut in the quotas. Italian immigration fell from 42,057 before the war to 3,845, Poles from 30,977 to 5,982, and Turks from 2,654 to 100. The new law granted many nations only 100 migrants a year.

Never before had an American government manipulated its statistics and dates to curtail immigration. By relying on its carefully designated dates and statistics, Congress sought to hide its effort to favor certain ethnic peoples over others. But the hand of bigotry was obvious and fueled animosity toward innocent ethnic minorities who came from the "wrong" portion of Europe or from Asia.

The federal government also carried discrimination into new "intelligence tests" for immigrants that did not take into account their distinct cultures and languages. Increased red tape was placed in the way of foreigners who sought visas to the United States. To gain visas, families had to produce hard-to-find documents. A year after the new act passed, immigration again fell by 50 percent.

The new immigration laws did not affect people from Latin America or the Caribbean. Puerto Ricans and Virgin Islanders entered the continental United States as citizens of American possessions. People of color and others living in South American or Caribbean colonies of England and France entered under the large quotas allotted to these western European nations.

CHAPTER 10

IMMIGRATION RESTRICTION AND CONSEQUENCES

The discriminatory immigration laws were an outgrowth of racial bigotry manipulated by many American political leaders. In turn, the immigration quotas set by the Congress had the effect of spurring hatred by officially designating some ethnic groups as superior and others as inferior. This encouraged more intolerance toward people who only spoke a foreign language, spoke English with an accent, or had been born overseas. An entire generation was taught their parents had failed some kind of humanity test.

The new immigration laws also accelerated pressures for assimilation and Americanization of immigrants. In 1924 Minnesota teachers launched a "We Speak English" program for their Finnish American pupils. Students were told to ask parents to sign a pledge that read:

> We, the undersigned, believe that in order to be true
> Americans we must speak the language of America. We,
> therefore, pledge ourselves to speak English at school at
> all times, and at home as far as possible, and to encourage
> and teach others to do the same.

Children of immigrant families learned in school to reject old-world ways. One of the casualties of assimilation was the foreign language press. People who read in their original language died off, and few new ones replaced them. A second generation might know how to read the old language, but refused to. Parents felt rejected.

In 1914 the immigrant press was at its height with 1300 foreign language papers and periodicals being published, 40 percent in German. Over the next quarter century, the number fell to under a thousand, and by 1970, foreign language papers numbered only 75.

Each ethnic group struggled with generational problems. In 1922 Greek Americans formed The American Hellenic Educational Progressive Association (AHEPA) as a nonsectarian force for assimilation. It attracted businessmen and professionals who sought economic advancement. But the next year the Greek American Progressive Association (GAPA) formed to foster interest in Greece's language, church, and legacy and to oppose intermarriage and the abandonment of traditions. Some of these reactions arose from the stresses of the new immigration laws. By 1930, as Greek Americans tried to unite their factions and to Americanize, the debate over assimilation waned. Many young people had moved away from parents and old neighborhoods, and some had intermarried. Newspapers that once appeared in Greek, now were published in English.

The same was true of Latvian Americans. In 1930 they numbered 38,091, including 17,418 born in the U.S. Some 70 percent of new arrivals had become citizens or declared their intent to do so. Less than a third of all Latvian families in the United States still spoke Latvian, and even those born overseas sought to rapidly adapt to American thinking and ways.

Arab Americans quickly adapted to American business methods but more slowly to social demands. It took sheer determination for Arab Americans to build the first Melkite, Maronite, and Orthodox churches in the 1890s. By the early 1920s, 72 other Arab American churches had been erected in 28 states.

The American experience redirected the strong Arab sense of family, honor, and status. Muslim values such as generosity and hospitality linked up with the American race for material wealth. The Muslim belief in hard work and thrift fitted neatly into an American capitalist drive for profitable businesses.

Syrian Americans had formed many organizations. In 1932 when these societies met together in Boston, the leaders were English-speaking Arab Americans in business suits and ties.

Some 30,000 Armenians reached these shores between 1920 and 1930 with women 52 percent and children 21 percent of arrivals. New York City became their American mecca, but some newcomers settled in New England, Michigan, California, and Illinois. By 1930,

Sacco and Vanzetti

Animosity toward foreigners reached a high point in the case of Italian immigrants, Nicola Sacco, 29, a shoemaker, and Bartolomeo Vanzetti, 32, a fish peddler. In 1920 the two labor agitators were arrested during the Red Scare as they handed out leaflets protesting the death of a friend while in police custody.

Charges of "radical agitation" were dropped against the two. Instead Sacco and Vanzetti were tried for murders committed during two different Massachusetts payroll robberies, charges they vigorously denied.

Judge Webster Thayer, who presided at both trials, and the district attorney in the case played on the patriotism of the jury. Felix Frankfurter, later a Supreme Court Justice, described the trial in these words:

> By systematic exploitation of the defendants' alien blood, their imperfect knowledge of English, their unpopular social views, and their opposition to the war, the district attorney invoked against them a riot of political passion and patriotic sentiment; and the trial judge connived at [this].

Finally, another man admitted committing the crimes for which Sacco and Vanzetti had been found guilty and said they were innocent. But Judge Thayer denied the two a new trial. Public meetings from India to Spain to Argentina protested the verdict. But, in spite of this, in 1927 the two immigrant agitators were executed. ■

Nicola Sacco and Bartolomeo Vanzetti

Detroit with 3,508 Armenian Americans was second only to New York City, and "Little Armenias" had also sprouted in a dozen major cities.

Early Armenian American immigrant men and three-quarters of the women took American jobs in search of economic success. In 1920 Gullabi Gulbenkian used his business profits to start a foundation to promote higher education and church projects. Alex Manoogian, who fled Turkey at 19, invested in a manufacturing concern in Detroit that grew into the giant Masco Corporation.

The Japanese were completely excluded as immigrants, and Japanese Americans soon encountered new obstacles. In 1922 Congress' Cable Act revoked citizenship from any American who married "an alien ineligible to citizenship," meaning an Asian. Then the Supreme Court denied the citizenship application of Takao Ozawa when it ruled that naturalization "was confined to white persons." When California passed an Alien Land Law that forbid Japanese Americans to buy land even in the name of their *Nisei* or American-born children, Arizona passed a similar law, followed by New Mexico, Idaho, Montana, and Oregon.

Japanese Americans comprised only two percent of California's population, but they produced 13 percent of the state's crops. And this was despite the fact their farms averaged only 56 acres compared to a 320 acre average for white-owned farms. When whites boycotted their products, Japanese Americans began their own farmers' markets. In California alone they started 50 trade societies. But hard work and success, cherished in others, was viewed by many Californians as part of a Japanese menace.

Japanese Americans continued to demand justice. In 1930 Clarence Arai's Japanese American Citizens League (JACL) challenged the Cable Act and discrimination in general and sought citizenship for Japanese Americans who served in World War I. By then, Japanese Americans had been elected to office in Hawaii, and others had published the *Courier* newspaper in English in Seattle. In 1931 the JACL had as its first victory — an amendment to the Cable Act which allowed *Nisei* women to marry *Issei* men without losing their U.S. citizenship.

CHAPTER 11

NATIVE AMERICAN CULTURAL RESISTANCE

While the United States waged military battles against Native Americans for centuries, in the 20th century its weapon against Native Americans was "assimilation," an effort to destroy or dominate every aspect of Native American culture. Proud nations now waged a battle for the survival of their cultural heritage. First, federal officials sought to end their traditional common ownership of land by insisting that Indians become farmers or ranchers. Native Americans in the process soon lost two-thirds of their land. The government continued to send Indian children to boarding schools far from their parents, where white educators tried to eradicate their languages and cultural legacies.

Throughout the first decades of the 20th century, Native American resistance, though no longer violent, took active forms. People struggled successfully to preserve their ancient ways, and, of hundreds of Indian languages, only a dozen died out. Assaults on their traditional customs led to vigorous campaigns by Native Americans to retain their rituals, ceremonies, and religious rites.

Native Americans found some sources of hope. The Mexican Revolution of 1910 offered bold government programs in Mexico that respected indigenous peoples. With the passing of the U.S. fron-

Native American children were taken from their parents and sent to boarding schools that tried to detach them from their cultures.

In 1918 Native Americans in Pueblo, New Mexico, made pottery.

tier, the white viewpoint that Native Americans were a barrier to be overcome also ended.

But the Bureau of Indian Affairs had committed itself to root out Native American culture. It feared that if left to themselves, Indians would "go back to the blanket" or return to former ways. Except among the Southwest's Navajo and Pueblo Indians which preserved their ancient forms of worship, Christianity became the dominant Native American religion. However, even Indian societies confined on reservations blended Christianity with the practices of their ancestors or created their own religious forms.

Native Americans also began to protest the way history texts pictured them as evil. In 1927 the Grand Council Fire of American Indians said to Chicago's mayor,

We do not know if school histories are pro-British, but we do know that they are unjust to the life of our people — the American Indian. They call all white victories, battles, and all Indian victories, massacres....

History books teach that Indians were murderers — is it murder to fight in self-defense: Indians killed white men because white men took their lands, ruined their hunting grounds, burned their forests, destroyed their buffalo. White men penned our people on reservations, then took away the reservations. White men who rise to protect their property are called patriots — Indians who do the same are called murderers.

In the 1920s Native Americans fought Congress' Bursum Bill that aimed to divide all remaining Native American assets among individuals. Indians did not believe in individual ownership and had always insisted that land was owned by the nation who used it. Reformer John Collier characterized the bill as "an orgy of loot" that spelled disaster for Native Americans: "...the pittance in money they would receive would scarcely have compensated for the loss of their homes and lands and tribal unities, the roots of both their individual and communal beings."

Pueblo Indian Alcario Montoya told his people, "We must unite as we did once before [the Pueblo revolt of 1680]." The Council of All the New Mexico Pueblos met for the second time in 242 years. At the council 123 people represented 19 Plains Indian nations. John Collier, one of three whites present, said the meeting gave him "a feeling of immensity. Far horizons seemed to stretch onward, and power seemed to flow from remote ages."

When Pueblo leaders sent 17 men to persuade Americans to defeat the bill, the Bureau of Indian Affairs called them thieves and "agents of communism." The bureau organized a competing Pueblo Council, and its agents spread gossip that tried to show that Pueblos were immoral. But, in 1923 with the aid of Senator Robert La Follette, the Bursum Bill was defeated.

Nevertheless, federal officials remained unrelenting in their assaults on Native American civilizations. In 1926 Indian Commissioner Charles Burke told Taos Pueblo leaders they were "half animals" who practiced "paganism." Pueblos were jailed for practicing ancient rituals. But they gained their release from a New Mexico prison when many whites protested this injustice.

Dr. Carlos Montezuma, Voice of Protest

Carlos Montezuma, a southwestern Indian, graduated from Northwestern Medical School in 1889 and became a Chicago physician. In 1915, speaking at the Society of American Indians, he called for abolition of the Bureau of Indian Affairs and its 11 million dollar budget, and dismissal of its 8,000 white employees. Dr. Montezuma said, "The only way to adjust wrong is to abolish it, and the only reform is to let my people go."

He continued:
In a free country we are not free. Wake up Indians, all over America. We are hoodwinked, duped more and more every year; we are made to feel that we are free when we are not. We are chained hand and foot; we stand helpless, innocently waiting for the fulfillment of promises that will never be fulfilled.... ∎

CHAPTER 12

THE GREAT DEPRESSION

In October 1929 the stock market crashed, and in two years banks failed, factories closed, and the United States sank into a major economic depression. During this "Great Depression," jobless men and women wandered around looking for work, and as each week passed with no luck, their clothes looked more ragged, and the situation became more desperate. City families, unable to pay their rent, were evicted from their apartments, and farm families lost their homes and land. By 1932, about 14 million American laborers woke up each morning without jobs.

"The depression," said poet Langston Hughes, "brought everybody down a peg or two." But it brought down people of color faster than most others since they were usually the last hired and first fired.

In St. Paul, Minnesota, more than three-quarters of the Mexican American population was on relief. Mexican American farm workers in the Southwest saw their wages fall from 31 cents an hour to 15 cents. Half of the 3 million Mexican Americans in the United States left for Mexico.

During the Great Depression, the jobless, such as these men in Pittsburgh, Pennsylvania, united to protest their condition.

Native Americans found that tourist visits to their reservations dropped drastically. Off the reservations, Native Americans could no longer find farm work or even other low-paying jobs.

Young Filipino Americans dropped out of high school and college. In Los Angeles the Filipino Social Relief Service could not feed all the jobless Filipino Americans because as one wrote, "So many came — often as many as 300 in one day."

Jobs for African Americans evaporated. In Baltimore African Americans made up

17 percent of the total population but 32 percent of the jobless. In Chicago the black 4 percent of the population comprised 32 percent of the unemployed. In Pittsburgh, the black 8 percent of the population made up 38 percent of the jobless. In farming areas unemployment among people of color was even higher.

With rising unemployment it became easier to lay off women first. They would be hurt by joblessness, but, it was assumed, men rather than women were family breadwinners. In an effort to save jobs for men, large city school systems refused to hire married women as teachers. Women rarely appeared on breadlines or begged for food, but that did not mean their needs were met. A federal investigator in cities, Mary Anderson, found women who were "literally starving to death in cold garrets and other out-of-the-way places."

To the dismay of some immigrant parents, their children dropped out of school and college to seek work. Many young men and some young women hitchhiked on the open road or boarded empty cattle cars to search for full- or part-time jobs.

The hard times accelerated the movement from country to city. This dislocation ended the rural isolation that had acted as a kind of glue for ethnic cohesion, pride, and survival. For example, Czech Americans who left for cities often did not settle among or associate with other Czech Americans. Men and women who embraced old-world ties in the country lost interest in these traditions as city dwellers. Foreign language newspapers continued their steep decline in numbers.

The depression years also spurred the growth of American popular culture. Radio and movies created a more national and homogeneous culture. Ethnic legacies had to compete with the new popular songs, movie actors, and swing bands. Cars and telephones meant a modern world not of ethnic isolation but of rapid communication and transportation. The universally popular culture offered the young new images of behavior, language, and ideas that began to replace those imposed by family traditions. Everywhere the media projected new American forms of music, dance, movies, and clothes that challenged the old.

The depression with its massive unemployment and uncertainty brought little violence between American ethnic groups. Conflict between national and racial groups actually slackened. The hard times seemed to renew a sense of national unity. It was clear that the middle class and the poor rural or urban classes were all suffering in the hard times. Men and women of every religion, ethnic group, and race stood on line in cities to receive a stale piece of bread or a cup of lukewarm soup.

A popular song of the day captured a new American unity: "We're in the Same Boat, Brother." In 1930 when some in Congress urged a huge cutback in immigration, Greek, Italian, Syrian, and Jewish Americans united in Boston to protest their action.

The restrictive laws of the 1920s had slowed immigration, and the depression virtually stopped it cold. In 1928 more than 300,000 people arrived in America from foreign shores, but by 1932, immigration had fallen to 23,000. Between 1930 and 1940, for the first time, the number of people who left the United States exceeded the number who entered the country.

The Ku Klux Klan hoped the depression would fatten their ranks, but this did not happen. The battle against the hard times also began to dent the walls of segregation. Unemployment Councils (UC) and Workers Alliances (WA) recruited men and women of every color, religion, and ethnic background. "Black and white, unite and fight!" became a popular sign carried by protesters.

The most dramatic legal case of the decade brought many citizens to the defense of nine African American young men who had been arrested in Scottsboro, Alabama, in 1931. The nine youths were charged with the rape of two white women. On the women's testimony, the nine were found guilty and sentenced to death. A worldwide crusade was organized by Communists and then by the NAACP to win a new trial. Samuel Liebowitz, a noted Jewish American attorney, pleaded their case before the U.S. Supreme

In 1929 Steve Nelson, a Yugoslav immigrant (top right) was one of six men arrested for asking for unemployment insurance.

Labor agitator Mother Bloor (left) and the mothers of the Scottsboro youths marched in a protest parade.

Court and won a new trial. Then, in 1933 one of the women accusers admitted that she and her friend had lied about the rape. But, it was years before the last of the nine were released.

Interracial violence retreated in the 1930s. Although 100 African Americans were lynched in the South in this decade, this was a sharp drop over previous decades.

In Oklahoma City, black and white men and women joined together to raid a grocery store and carry off food for their hungry families. In Greenville, South Carolina, 2,000 men of both races marched to a building site to demand jobs. In Alabama, Communist Party members organized a black sharecropper's union that also recruited a few white members. The union often had to operate in secret, but it did publish and circulate a newspaper. Union meetings opened with a prayer and said little about communism.

A dramatic protest against the depression came in 1932 when 15,000 World War I veterans marched on Washington, D.C., to demand payment of a bonus promised by Congress. This "Bonus Army" united sons and grandsons of immigrants and slaves. In Houston, Texas, a multiracial delegation told how they "were served meals in Southern towns by white waitresses."

In 1932 the "Bonus Army" marched on Washington D.C., to ask for the government's help during the hard time.

In Washington, the Bonus Army set up tents for their families. Everywhere, wrote black reporter Roy Wilkins, African Americans "were in front, in the middle, and in the rear."

> There was no residential segregation.... The Chicago group had several hundred Negroes in it, and they worked, ate, slept, and played with their white comrades. The Negroes shared tasks with the whites from kitchen work to camp M.P. duty.

President Herbert Hoover authorized the U.S. Army to tear down the camps, and in a single day of army tear gas and bayonets, the veterans were driven from the capital. But this clash between the

*Congressman
Oscar De Priest*

president and the nation's wartime defenders turned many people against Hoover and his Republican Party, and later that year Hoover was swept out of the White House.

But the winds of political change had begun earlier. In 1928 the first African American congressman of the 20th century, and the first from a northern state, Republican Oscar De Priest, was elected from Chicago.

De Priest urged black voters to change America through politics:

> You will never be able to get what you want politically unless you elect leaders who will fight for your interest.... White people as a rule elect Negroes that they can control. Negroes never get a square deal unless you elect your own leaders....

Multiethnic Figures Elected to Office

Before President Hoover left office, American ethnic groups had elected their candidates to some important state and local offices. In 1928 Octaviano Larrazolo, born in Mexico in 1859, was elected to the U.S. Senate from New Mexico. He had a long and distinguished political career, and he became the first Mexican American governor of New Mexico.

In 1930 Julius Meyer, who was a Jewish American, was elected governor of Oregon. The next year Angelo Rossi, son of a Genoese immigrant, was elected mayor of San Francisco, an office he held until 1944. In 1932 Jewish American Louis Marcus was elected mayor of Salt Lake City, Utah.

In 1932 Democrat Anton Cermak, an immigrant from Kladno, a Czech coal mining town, was elected Chicago's first foreign-born mayor. He had successfully united many people in the city's various ethnic communities behind his candidacy. Sitting in a car with President-elect Franklin D. Roosevelt in Miami, Florida, the next year, Cermak was shot and killed when someone tried to assassinate Roosevelt.

In 1932 Herbert Lehman, in the landslide election that brought FDR to the White House, was elected as the first Jewish governor of New York and was reelected three more times. That same year O. Melena in Pennsylvania became the first Lithuanian American elected to a state legislature. In 1932 Minnesota sent five Norwegian Americans and two Swedish Americans to Congress. ∎

Mayor Anton Cermak

Letter from a Veteran

In January 1931 *The Negro Worker* printed a letter from an "Unemployed Negro Ex-Soldier" in Atlanta, Georgia. He wrote:

> Am unemployed for 8 months. Was a soldier in the world war where I fought for [President] Wilson's equality and democracy for Negroes. Because of the wounds received in battle, I cannot get a job. They want younger fellows who they work like the devil for nothing at all.
>
> The city here opened up a Community Kitchen dump. Every day, hundreds of employed, starving Negroes and whites go there with their two cents to get a can of slop. But the Negroes, because of the discrimination there, are not going any longer. They would rather starve than be insulted as they are down there.
>
> When a Negro does get past the insulting red tape and question cards he got to fill out, then he finds that he must have two cents and a tin can in order to get a cupful of stinking mixed vegetables and a hunk of stale bread, while whites get their choice of soup or milk and even some of them have coal delivered to their home.
>
> The Negroes are not putting up with these miserable conditions and are organizing into the League of Struggle for Negro Rights, to fight discrimination of all kinds, off the job and on the job. ∎

With the interethnic unity forged by the depression, minorities moved more easily into positions of political power. In the months following the stock market crash, President Hoover appointed two Jewish Americans to high government posts. He asked Eugene Meyer to serve on the Federal Reserve Board and appointed Benjamin Cardozo to the U.S. Supreme Court where he joined Louis Brandeis, the court's first Jewish American Supreme Court Justice who had been appointed by President Wilson.

Minorities found there was power in protest. In 1931 President Hoover nominated John J. Parker of North Carolina to the Supreme Court. Parker had previously opposed voting rights for African Americans, so the NAACP denounced Parker and, since the judge also held antiunion views, the AFL joined the attack. This coalition convinced the Senate to reject Parker's nomination.

PRESIDENT ROOSEVELT AND THE NEW DEAL

In the election year of 1932 the economic depression reached its depths. Stock market prices had fallen to 11 percent of their 1929 value, and the national suicide rate had doubled. President Hoover called his Democratic opponent, Franklin Delano Roosevelt, an "innovator," but people wanted an innovator. FDR carried 42 states to Hoover's 6.

By Inauguration Day, the nation seemed under siege. Some city schools had been suspended, some businesses could not meet payrolls, and many customers could not pay for groceries. Three-fourths of the states had closed their banks.

In his inauguration speech, Roosevelt tried to sound confident and optimistic. "Our great primary task is to put people to work," he said. "The only thing we have to fear is fear itself."

The new president had some untried ideas about how to solve the economic crisis. Privately he wondered if his experiments would work. He proposed a "New Deal" in which the federal government would play a direct role in economic life. For these innovations to be successful, he needed to unify a nation of many racial, ethnic, and religious groups during a terrible time.

In 1939 President Roosevelt met with famous African American scientist George Washington Carver in Tuskegee, Alabama.

The new president and particularly his wife, Eleanor, repeatedly reached out to ethnic groups and denounced bigotry. FDR told the conservative Daughters of the American Revolution: "Remember, remember always, that all of us, and you and I especially, are descended from immigrants and revolutionists." In 1935 FDR declared October 9 Leif Erikson Day to honor this Scandinavian explorer of the New World, and in 1937 the president wrote to the Syrian American Society of South Carolina warmly praising their "distinctive contribution to our social, political, and economic life." In 1938 at Arlington National Cemetery he honored the greatest Polish American hero of the Civil War.

One of the president's strongest supporters in Congress was Robert F. Wagner who served in the U.S. Senate from 1927 to 1949. He was born in Germany in 1875 and had come to the U. S. at age 10. A leading New Dealer, Wagner had sponsored Roosevelt's National Industrial Recovery Act and Social Security Act. Wagner also wrote the National Labor Relations Law, known as the Wagner Act.

FDR enjoyed enormous and spontaneous popularity among minorities. In 1939 when he came to Manhattan to dedicate a tunnel to the borough of Queens, a Syrian American mother broke through police lines to shake his hand. As secret service agents surrounded her, she reached into her shopping bag and handed the president a jar of homemade fruit jam "for the next time you have company at the White House."

Eleanor Roosevelt became one of the most acclaimed women of the century. She was the first presidential wife to appear in public with African Americans and to endorse racial equality. In 1934 Eleanor Roosevelt appeared at a White House costume party wearing an authentic Romanian peasant dress created for her by a noted authority of Romanian folkways, Anisoara Stan.

Roosevelt's New Deal appointments opened doors that had once been closed to ethnic groups. Irish Americans rose rapidly to high office beginning with FDR's first choice as attorney general, Thomas Walsh of Montana who had been a champion of civil liberties. The postmaster was James Farley, the Irish American politician who had directed Roosevelt's election campaign.

New Deal cabinet appointments also broke other barriers. FDR selected Henry Morganthau, Jr., a Jewish American, as his secretary

Frances Perkins became the first woman to sit in a presidential cabinet.

Robert Weaver was part of FDR's "Black Cabinet."

Mary McLeod Bethune was a good friend and advisor to Eleanor Roosevelt and FDR.

of the treasury, and Morganthau held the position through all four FDR terms. Samuel Rosenman, a Jewish American New York judge, was one of FDR's closest advisors and speech writers.

In 1936 Matthew T. Abruzzo of New York City was appointed as the first federal judge of Italian descent. That same year Miecislaus Szuymcak was made a governor of the Federal Reserve Bank making him the top Polish American federal appointee. In 1939 FDR put Felix Frankfurter on the Supreme Court and made another Jewish American, Ernest Greuning, the governor of the Alaska Territory.

One of the president's most daring appointments was Frances Perkins as secretary of labor, the first woman to sit in a presidential cabinet. She was a social worker at Hull House in Chicago and a seasoned state factory inspector in New York. She campaigned for a five-day week, a minimum wage for all, and abolition of child labor. She was the first cabinet member in history to urge "gradually raising the living standards of the colored laborers."

From his first year on, the president and his leading officials relied on a "Black Cabinet," a group of prominent African Americans who served as advisors on racial issues. The Black Cabinet met in the basement of Robert Weaver's Washington home to plan their strategy. Weaver later was chosen as the first African American cabinet member by President Lyndon Johnson.

The Black Cabinet's William Hastie later became a governor of the Virgin Islands and a federal judge. Another member, Ralph Bunche, served in the State Department. Later, as a UN leader, he became the first African American to win the Noble Peace Prize.

Educator Mary McLeod Bethune who began Bethune-Cookman College in 1904 with a few dollars of her own also was a member of the Black Cabinet. She served as an advisor to presidents Roosevelt and Truman. FDR once told Bethune he was always happy to see her "for you always come asking for help for others — never for yourself." The Black Cabinet urged ending segregation and proposed many ways of handling racial friction. Their views were heard, but their advice was not often used.

Women made economic advances under New Deal programs. In 1933 almost half a million women, mostly widows, single women, and women married to unemployed men, worked for the federal government's Works Projects Administration (WPA) that provided work for jobless men and women.

Minimum wages for women in interstate commerce remained below those paid to men, but some New Deal measures helped narrow the salary gap between the sexes. For example, men's wages in the shoe industry were set at 35 cents an hour, and women's at 30 cents. Because so many women worked in domestic service, agriculture, and as professionals, they were not covered by such New Deal laws as minimum wage or social security.

Wild Mustard

Frank Murphy, who was born in 1890 to an Irish American family and came from a fighting tradition, rose high in the New Deal. A tall, thin young man with dark red hair, Murphy attended college and law school and was nicknamed "Wild Mustard." He taught night classes in English to Hungarian immigrants. He served in the U.S. Army during World War I and at 25 became a captain.

Murphy took part in revolutionary activity in Ireland after the war and then returned home to Detroit. As a federal district attorney, he busted rackets and brought criminals to trial. Appointed a Detroit judge, he earned a reputation for fairness when he presided over the Sweet case in which Blacks defended their home from a white mob.

In 1930 Murphy was elected mayor of Detroit and used his position to draw attention to the depression's homeless and starving. He stated his belief in liberalism in these words:

The enlightened administrator must put his very soul into the fight to guard against undernourished children, neglected old folks, and victimized wage workers. He must plan, yes, but mere plans and words are not enough. He must act, and his acts must be written into the statutes in the form of old-age pensions, better factory laws, and general social legislation; they must be in brick and stone in the shape of hospitals for children; they must be in dollars and cents and bread and butter in the form of relief and succor for employees, victims of an unemployment they did not create.

In 1936 Murphy was elected governor of Michigan. He refused to help corporations crush strikes with state troops and instead helped settle the famous 1937 Detroit auto strike peacefully.

In 1938 President Roosevelt appointed Murphy as U.S. attorney general. In 1940 Murphy was appointed to the U.S. Supreme Court where he served with distinction until his death in 1949. ■

CHAPTER 14

NEW DEAL POLITICS

The spirit of national unity and New Deal experimentalism helped a host of women and minority candidates to gain high public office. By 1931, there were nine women serving in Congress, although five had inherited their husbands seats in the House. However, Hattie Carraway of Arkansas, appointed upon her husband's death, was elected in her own right in 1932. Another highly placed woman official was Nellie Taylor Ross, a former governor of Wyoming, who was appointed the U.S. treasurer.

The election of 1932 that swept FDR into the White House also brought a host of Irish Americans to the Senate, including Ryan Duffy of Wisconsin, Augustine Lonergan of Connecticut, and Pat McCarren of Nevada. Two years later Nebraska sent Edward Burke, and Wyoming sent Joseph O'Mahoney to the Senate.

Mayor Fiorello La Guardia presided over multicultural New York City.

In 1933 in New York City, Fiorello La Guardia, who was born to an Italian father and a Jewish mother, was elected mayor of New York City. La Guardia had campaigned in Yiddish, English, and Italian and had run for office on a "balanced ticket" — one that included candidates of Italian, Jewish, Irish, and Anglo-Protestant descent.

That same year Edward Corsi, an Italian immigrant, was appointed the United States Commissioner of Immigration and Naturalization. In the Hawaii Territory that year Tomekichi Okino became the first Japanese American appointed to a federal judgeship.

In 1935 Ukrainian American S. Jarema was elected to the New York State legislature, and the next year John S. Gonas was elected in Indiana. By 1936, 9 *Nisei* were among the 93 officials elected to office in Hawaii. In 1937 Solomon Blatt, a Jewish American, was picked as the Speaker of the South Carolina Assembly.

The New Deal congressional sweep in 1934 brought Arthur Mitchell of Illinois, the first African American Democrat, to Congress, and he served five terms. Mitchell replaced De Priest, and his victory symbolized a black urban shift to the Democratic Party. An outspoken critic of racial and religious bigotry, Mitchell successfully sued a railroad over segregation in 1942 and won.

Some Lithuanian Americans gained public office during the New Deal including two legislators in Pennsylvania, one in Illinois, and a Michigan judge. J. Kairis became mayor of Seatonville, Illinois, Anna Lakawitz, mayor of Linndale, Ohio, and J. Vansavage mayor of New Philadelphia, Pennsylvania.

In 1939 Stanley Nowak, born in 1903 in Austrian Poland, who at age 10 emigrated to Chicago, was elected to the Michigan State Senate and served for ten years. In the 1930s he had been an organizer of eastern European laborers in Detroit for the United Auto Workers Union and was among the first to seek union recruits over an ethnic radio station. Nowak became a founder of the American Slav Congress.

In 1934 Vito Marcantonio, born to immigrant Italian parents, was elected to Congress from East Harlem in New York City and served until 1950. He spoke out for unity among his district's Italian American, Puerto Rican, and African American residents. In 1949 he told a huge rally of his Italian American constituents:

> Yes, I do defend the Puerto Ricans as our most recently arrived, against the kind of discrimination that was practiced against the Irish, the Jews, and the Italians in the past.

In 1937 Marcantonio helped Oscar Garcia gain a seat in the New York State legislature and become the first Puerto Rican American elected to state office in the continental United States.

Flamboyant Mayor

Fiorello La Guardia was born in 1882 in New York City to an Italian father and an Italian Jewish mother from Trieste. Young Fiorello grew up in Arizona where the suffering of Native Americans and exploitation of Mexican and Italian American railroad laborers inspired him to help when he grew up.

He returned to New York, studied law, and worked at Ellis Island. Elected to Congress, La Guardia wrote the Norris-La Guardia Act of 1931 that finally freed unions from the court injunctions that employers used for decades to wreck strikes.

La Guardia began running for mayor of New York City in 1921 and finally was elected in 1933. For the next 12 years the peppery little man in the dark suit ran the city and influenced politics throughout the country. He used the radio to explain his views, and during a newspaper strike, he read the comics to the city's children. His critics said La Guardia tried to answer every letter he received and visit every major fire. The mayor laughed and said these were not criticisms.

La Guardia found a city deep in corruption, crying for political reform, and without enough playgrounds for children. He demanded action. Under his administrations, corruption was reduced, a new City Charter passed, slums were cleared, health and sanitation improved, and new parks and playgrounds were built.

La Guardia spoke to New Yorkers in some of their many languages and once boasted he could beat his enemies "running on a laundry ticket." He loved his city and its citizens, and they elected him four times. He was the first New York mayor to appoint people of color to city posts and the first to be a national political force.

La Guardia admitted his errors. "When I make a mistake," he said, "it's a beaut!" Emotional and hard-working, impatient and happy, even his foes felt his heart was in the right place. As mayor of the world's largest city, he set standards for honest, caring urban management for people rather than special interests.

La Guardia was a legend in his own time. In 1945 he chose not to run for mayor again. The next year he was appointed director of the new United Nation's Relief and Rehabilitation Administration where he was in charge of providing the people of the world with the basic necessities of life. He died at his UN post in 1947. ■

C H A P T E R   1 5

RACE AND THE NEW DEAL

The Roosevelt administration did not directly challenged racism. Federal agencies provided relief in a way that gave people of color fewer benefits than other Americans. The industrial code of the National Recovery Act (NRA) mandated higher salaries for whites than nonwhites. Less than 10 percent of home owner loans went to African Americans, and less than 10 percent of southern education aid went to schools for African Americans.

New Deal agencies handed jobs to whites first and made sure they were promoted over people of color. The Works Progress Administration (WPA) employed millions, but whites received more and African Americans fewer jobs than their respective percentages of the unemployed. The WPA built many schools but in segregated neighborhoods. About one-third of federally supported housing went to people of color, but almost all of this was segregated.

The Tennessee Valley Authority (TVA) brought cheap electricity to Appalachia, but most people of color could not afford its lower rates. Black journalist John P. Davis toured TVA projects where he found African Americans were hired only for unskilled jobs.

Black men found jobs in CCC camps.

African American southern sharecroppers and tenant farmers received cash benefits but rarely served on the government boards that handed out the checks. The poorest farm workers lost their jobs in the South, and this usually meant black people.

Sometimes discrimination was built into the best New Deal laws. For example, the Social Security Act, by excluding domestic and agricultural laborers from its benefits, eliminated most people of color and most women who worked.

Despite its failures, the New Deal era was one of great hope for women and people of color. The Civil Service Commission opened federal jobs to qualified people regardless of sex or race. By 1939, one-fifth of all civil service jobs were held by women, and they were paid the same wage as the men who worked beside them. Some 200,000 young black men joined the Civilian Conservation Corp which provided forestry work for young people, but only 30,000 of these served in integrated CCC camps.

The WPA taught 400,000 African American women and men to read and write. It hired many hungry, jobless women and African American artists, scholars, and actors. "Without that aid," recalled artist Ernest Critchlow, "many of today's important artists might never have made their contributions to the nation's art."

The WPA produced plays in English, Spanish, Yiddish, and French. It hired men and women to research their ethnic histories in various states and cities. A torrent of books were issued with such titles as *The Negro in Virginia* and *The Italians of New York*.

The hard times and the New Deal brought a new spirit to the oppressed. Black Alabama sharecroppers and tenant farmers who faced starvation began to stand up for their rights.

Interracial unions began to grow during the 1930s.

In Tallapoosa County, Alabama schoolteacher Estelle Milner and two brothers Tommy and Ralph Gray organized a black Croppers and Farm Workers Union and recruited 800 African Americans.

In July 1931, the union was resisting a reign of terror launched by lawmen, and it held out. In August the union reorganized as a Share Croppers Union (SCU), and Eula Gray, 19, was their leader for the next 9 months. Under her guidance 591 men and women were enrolled in 28 locals, 10 youth groups, and 12 women's auxiliaries.

Then under Al Murphy, a more experienced unionist, members arrived at meetings armed and assembled a small arsenal. Women unionists discussed labor conditions, formulated policies, and proved indispensable to the SCU. "Their organizing skills and basic concerns," reported historian Robin Kelley, "were the foundation of union activity."

In 1932 the SCU had 600 members. It received financial and moral support from Montgomery residents, women reformers, and some men led by Rabbi Benjamin Goldstein of Temple Beth Or.

Murphy saw that his SCU membership was rising. By June 1933, he had 2,000 members in 73 locals and by 1934, 8,000. That year the SCU ended its secrecy, led a successful cotton field strike, and began branches in Louisiana and Mississippi. Some poor white men and white women began to attend meetings, but none dared join the union.

By 1936, the SCU claimed 10,000 to 12,000 members and opened a public headquarters in New Orleans. The union was not defeated by racist attacks or violence but finally faded from the scene. It fell victim to the mechanization of southern agriculture. Some SCU members joined the National Farmers Union and other unions, and some remained in the SCU into World War II.

Together American and foreign-born, black, white, and brown men and women united to demand relief from the hard times. James Yates, born in Quitman, Mississippi, in 1906 had not associated with whites until he reached Chicago as a young man. He listened to radical speakers and joined a protest march on the Illinois capital at Springfield. He later wrote about that march:

> I caught the fever and found myself singing with a
> passion I hadn't felt for years.... I shivered with pleasure.
> Suddenly I felt as one with these people, Black and white.
> I was part of their hopes, their dreams, and they were part
> of mine. And we were part of an even larger world of
> marching poor people. By now, I understood that the
> depression was worldwide and that the unemployed and
> poor were demonstrating and agitating for jobs and food
> all over the globe. My throat swelled with pride. I sang
> loud enough for all Chicago to hear.

The march built in numbers and intensity and then was assaulted by Illinois National Guard troops using tear gas and clubs. Told to shield the women and not fight back, Yates was badly

73

beaten. But he had learned a lesson: "I had now experienced the power of the state." For Yates and others who had had similar experiences, there was no turning back, and some actively organized others to push for economic and political justice. Yates became a union organizer and a radical.

In Arkansas in 1935 Socialists, black sharecroppers, and some whites formed a Southern Tenant Farmers Union (STFU) that signed up 30,000 members. Blacks became union leaders since their church experience had given them more organizational experience than white members. White organizational experience had largely been in the Ku Klux Klan. The hard times had helped bring together African Americans and Klansmen in Arkansas.

In 1939 contralto Marion Anderson was denied the right to sing in Constitution Hall in Washington, D.C., which was owned by the Daughters of the American Revolution. A national protest was led by Harold Ickes, the New Deal secretary of the interior, and Eleanor Roosevelt. Ickes arranged for Anderson to sing from the Lincoln Memorial on Easter Sunday. An audience of 75,000 heard her sing operatic arias, folk music, and conclude with "America the Beautiful." Anderson recalled that moment:

Marion Anderson sang at the Lincoln Memorial to protest her exclusion from Constitution Hall.

The crowd stretched in a great semicircle from the Lincoln Memorial around the reflecting pool onto the shaft of the Washington Monument. I had a feeling that a great wave of goodwill poured out from these people, almost engulfing me.

In 1933 President Roosevelt appointed reformer John Collier as his Indian commissioner and ordered that special Indian CCC camps provide jobs for the young Native Americans. Collier worked with Native Americans to devise a plan that returned lands taken away by the federal government's allotment policy. Collier, the first commissioner to say Indian governments "must be given status, responsibility, and power," sought to return democratic rights to these proud nations.

By 1934, Collier had convinced Congress to pass an Indian

The Fighting Nurse

African American Salaria Kea was born in 1917, and she and her three brothers were orphaned at an early age. But the young woman was a fighter. When she was denied a place on her school's basketball team, she transferred to another school. In 1933, at age 16, she enrolled as a student at Harlem Hospital's School of Nursing. Later, as an obstetric nurse, she had to run the maternity-nursery ward of 50 babies by herself.

Kea led a revolt against the hospital dining room that, in the middle of Harlem, segregated black from white staff members. She and five other nurses refused to leave a table reserved "for whites only." Refused service, they rose and yanked the tablecloth so everything on it fell to the floor. "Everyone in the dining room was upset," she later wrote. "We demanded to see the superintendent of nurses. She arrived shortly, much excited."

Spearheaded by Kea's dynamism, the nurses won support from doctors. When Kea carried her heated protest into that year's election for mayor, she found that segregation "was abolished in one day." In 1935 when Benito Mussolini's Fascist armies invaded Ethiopia, Kea and other Harlem nurses collected and sent tons of medical supplies and a 75-bed hospital to the African nation. But Mussolini's air force and troops overwhelmed the unarmed Ethiopians before she and others completed plans to travel to the war zone.

The next year Spain was invaded by a rebel army led by General Francisco Franco and aided by Nazi Germany and Fascist Italy. This time Kea was ready. She said, "I'm not going to sit down and let this happen. I'm going to go out even if it means my life." In Spain, Kea and her medical team opened the first crude American base hospital near the Madrid front. An enemy air raid wrecked the hospital, and Kea, though buried in the rubble, survived.

Kea returned to the United States and made a cross-country speaking tour to raise money for the Spanish Republic. In World War II she served as a U.S. Army nurse and became a lieutenant. She died at 74 in 1990. ■

Salaria Kea

Reorganization Act that provided Indian self-rule and an end to the allotment system. The plan rested on the approval of Native Americans, and three-fourths of the nations voted to accept it. The Navajos and the 76 others who rejected it feared that it still gave the Department of the Interior too much power over Indian resources.

Collier further saw that federal loans spurred agricultural and industrial growth on reservations. He closed down 16 federally operated boarding schools that educated children away from their parents and replaced them with 84 reservation day schools.

Collier's policies gave Indians student loans and job preferences in the Bureau of Indian Affairs. His projects included irrigation, land conservation and restoration, herd management, reforestation, and the right of Native Americans to sell their crafts to the public for profit.

By World War II, Native American cattle holdings had increased by 105 percent and the production of animal products by 2,300 percent. The Native American mortality rate decreased by 55 percent. Collier wrote:

> We have watched scores of ancient tribal systems reorient
> themselves toward modern tasks, while more than a
> hundred tribal democracies have been newly born and
> have lived and marched out into life; these democracies
> are political, industrial, and social....

FILIPINO AMERICAN LABOR

When their islands were taken from Spain after the Spanish-American War by the United States, Filipinos became American nationals but not U.S. citizens. However, as American nationals, they could enter the United States freely not as foreigners. Many took jobs in Hawaii.

There were 5,603 Filipinos — they called themselves "Pinoys" — on the U.S. mainland in 1920. By the time of the Great Depression, there were 45,208 Filipinos in the United States. Most lived in California, but thousands had settled in Washington, Oregon, Illinois, and New York, with others in Kansas, Arizona, Montana, Mississippi, and Michigan.

Working 6-day weeks, 12 hours a day, Filipino Americans became 15 percent of the labor force hired by Alaskan fisheries. About 80 percent of those who came to California were men in their twenties. Wherever they found jobs, they were paid less than white labor and had to work longer hours. They also met racial discrimination. "I shall never forget what I have suffered in this country because of racial prejudice," wrote a Filipino scholar of United States institutions.

Filipino men invariably came to the United States alone to find work. "We would not have led miserable lives, nor drifted from one shoulder to another, if, in the beginning, our women had come with us," recalled one man. But the Filipino men were limited to farm or service jobs. A Filipino referred to America as "a beautiful lady surrounded with swords."

Filipino contractors brought labor crews from one U.S. farm to another. The farm workers labored in fields of strawberries, fruits, asparagus, and spinach in California, beets in Montana, potatoes in Idaho, apples in Washington, and hops in Oregon. Bosses preferred single Filipino men to Mexican American families who needed more housing.

Filipino men sweltered for hours in dry, dusty, hot fields and their skin became unbearably itchy, but one state official said: "The white man can't stand the itch.... The dark-skinned peoples are not affected by these conditions."

In 1933 the California Supreme Court decided that Filipinos were "Mongolian" and, therefore, could be legally barred from marrying whites. In a few years a dozen states made similar rulings. One Filipino American concluded:

The Americans are stupid when it comes to understanding foreign people because they think of themselves at their best and of foreigners at their worst. They do not take any time to stop and think that foreigners, especially my people, have a different psychology and civilization.

Filipino Americans often met signs on hotels reading "Positively No Filipinos Allowed." Landlords said, "Only whites are allowed in this neighborhood." Barbers refused to cut their hair, and some theaters denied them entrance.

In the 1920s Filipino laborers gained a reputation for arguing over wages and for going on strike. A decade later bosses described them as "educated and sophisticated" and "hard to manage."

White workers, fearful of job competition in 1930, threw a dynamite bomb into a camp of about a hundred sleeping Filipino American workers in Reedly, California. Filipino Americans responded by carrying guns to work.

When Filipino men began to attend local dances to find dates, this stirred further white fears. A letter to a California paper complained about Filipino men who believe they have "a perfect right to mingle with the white people and even to intermarry."

For Filipino Americans conditions worsened during the New Deal. In 1934 the Tydings-McDuffie Act made the Philippines a commonwealth to be granted independence in ten years. But the act's other purpose, said Maryland senator Millard Tydings, was to exclude Filipinos from the United States claiming their presence would increase "racial prejudice and bad feelings of all kinds." The new law denied Filipinos federal relief, jobs, or any other kind of government aid.

Carlos Bulosan

Carlos Bulosan was born in 1911 to a Philippine farm family in Luzon. In 1930 he came to Seattle to find his two brothers who left home earlier. He did locate them. Bulosan, who could read and write, wanted to complete his education and become a writer. Like many Filipinos, he planned to return home, but never did.

Bulosan worked in Alaskan fish canneries and picked apples in Washington and oranges in California. He took odd jobs in Montana, Texas, and New Mexico. He was a dishwasher and a houseboy, and he was often unemployed. He once robbed a man at gunpoint, and he also stole a ring from a house.

Bulosan was turned away from hotels and stores. "We don't take Filipinos," a landlady told Bulosan and his brother Marcario. The two men finally found a home on Hope Street in Los Angeles.

It was a noisy and tragic street, where suicides and murders were a daily occurrence, but it was the only place in the city where we could find a home. There was no other district where we were allowed to reside.

Once Bulosan and other Filipino American laborers were beaten by whites in Washington's Yakima Valley. In Oregon he was arrested by two policemen who called him a "brown monkey." When he and a friend tried to organize a union, a white mob held them at gunpoint, and stripped and beat them.

But Bulosan also found white women and men who were kind and helpful, gave him books, and encouraged his education. During the depression, he found himself identifying with persecuted groups such as African Americans and Jewish Americans. He concluded:

America is not a land of one race or one class of men. We are all Americans that have toiled and suffered and known oppression and defeat.... America is also the nameless foreigner, the homeless refugee, the hungry boy begging for a job.... America is the illiterate immigrant who is ashamed that the world of books and intellectual opportunities is closed to him.

Bulosan organized unions, wrote for "voiceless farm workers," and tried to inspire Filipino Americans and others who faced discrimination. He wrote of a cannery workers' meeting in San Pedro in which "Japanese, Mexicans, Filipinos, and white Americans" spoke out "in broken English, but always with sincerity and passion." He believed that the United States "was an unfinished dream." In 1946 Carlos Bulosan wrote his autobiography, *America Is in the Heart*. By 1956, when he died, he had also written and published books of poems, essays, and short stories. ■

Finally, in 1935 Congress passed a law to send Filipinos to their homeland at federal expense if they agree not to return. Less than 2,200 people accepted this repatriation. During the New Deal years, Filipino migration to the United States dropped by 90 percent.

In 1930 Julian Ilar, a Chicago University student, wrote of his people's efforts to assimilate into American culture:

> Try as we will we cannot become Americans. We may go to the farthest extreme in our effort to identify ourselves with the ways of the Americans, straightening our noses, dressing like the American in the latest fashion, pasting our faces with bleaching cream and our hair with [other creams] — but nevertheless we are not able to shake off that tenacious psychology.

In Stockton and Salinas, California, during the depression, a Filipino Labor Union formed with the slogan "Strength is in union." By 1934, the FLU led 6,000 lettuce workers on a work stoppage that was joined by whites who packed and stored the gathered lettuce.

Furious growers hired Mexicans as strikebreakers, claimed that Communists had seized the FLU, and convinced state police and deputies to drive off the strikers. Vigilantes attacked and burned the main FLU camp, and deputies jailed FLU leader Rufo Canete. But FLU members held out and finally won wages of 40 cents an hour and recognition for their union. In 1936 one FLU strike in the Salinas Valley successfully united Mexican and Filipino Americans.

Filipino American lettuce pickers in 1939.

CHAPTER 17

MEXICAN AMERICANS CONFRONT HARD TIMES

With simple eloquence a Mexican American writer told how his people, who got little federal aid, fared during the depression:

> We waited in long relief lines. We organized and
> protested. We went hungry — hungrier than usual.

To avoid caring for jobless Mexicans, the federal government deported 300,000 people to Mexico. Mexican American relatives of the deported then also left. The Great Depression drove additional thousands of people back across the Rio Grande.

Those who remained during the New Deal faced a segregated educational system in which more than half of Mexican American pupils were usually in the first three grades, and few attended high school or college. Mexican Americans often had the highest illiteracy rate of any American ethnic group. But a California university's study of Los Angeles' Jefferson High School did not blame the school system:

In 1937 Mexican Americans living in St. Paul, Minnesota, celebrated Mexican Independence Day.

The Mexicans, as a group, lack ambition. The peon of Mexico has spent so many generations in a condition of servitude that a lazy acceptance of his lot has become a racial characteristic.

Official indifference to Mexican Americans was common. In one county the state listed 80 percent of Mexican American deaths as due to "unknown causes." In some towns rickets, a disease caused by lack of calcium and common among poor people, soared to 84 percent. An average of 40 percent of children born to Mexican American parents did not live to become adults.

Mexican American families remained strong through an abiding faith in Catholicism and the conviction that relatives and neighbors would help defeat adversity. For children, life had many happy moments. Henry Garcia, born in Tucson, Arizona, recalled the fun he shared with other ethnic groups in his *barrio*:

We all lived together — there was a mixture of people — Jews, Syrians, naturally many Mexicans, Chinese, Lebanese — and everyone spoke Spanish.

Garcia told how women in his community visited over the fence and "a boy could have a lot of adventures." He recalled:

I saw a lot of things and learned a lot. There were a lot of fiestas. Anytime there was a baptism or birthday there was a fiesta. There was always music.

Mexican American strikers in California were prepared for violence.

During the New Deal, Mexican Americans continued to form unions. By 1933, 50,000 Mexican American farm laborers in California organized 50 local unions. Soon, other Mexican American farm unions were started in Arizona, Texas, New Mexico, and Colorado.

In 1933, 7,000 of the Mexican American farm laborers struck the berry, onion, and celery fields of

Los Angeles County. Strikes spread to Mexican American cannery workers, cotton workers, and pea pickers.

Employer violence was so widespread that Senator Robert La Follette's Senate Committee investigated companies that had used force in defiance of the law. The testimony of one deputy sheriff revealed the racist beliefs of white lawmen:

> Mexicans are trash. They have no standard of living. We
> herd them like pigs.

Strikes grew even more violent. In 1936, 1,500 California police battled Mexican American strikers. Later that year 2,500 Mexican American citrus field-workers in Orange County went on strike, lawmen were issued shoot-to-kill orders, and the Los Angeles Times reported that the "old vigilante days were revived."

Meanwhile, strikes spread to other states. In 1934 in Texas, San Angelo Mexican American sheepshearers walked off their jobs, and in 1938 in San Antonio pecan shellers went on strike. *Nation* editor Carey McWilliams found strikes erupting in Arizona, Idaho, Texas, Washington, Colorado, and Michigan," wherever Mexicans were employed in agriculture." He concluded:

> With scarcely an exception, every strike in which
> Mexicans participated in the borderlands in the thirties
> was broken by the use of violence and was followed by
> deportations. In most of these strikes, Mexican workers
> stood alone; that is, they were not supported by organized
> labor....

Mexican American women eagerly joined strike activities since they too were overworked, underpaid, and often the sole support of large families. Mexican American women made up more than half of the Southwest's garment factory workers.

In 1938 when a thousand Mexican American men in 130 pecan shelling factories in San Antonio,Texas, struck to raise a wage of 5 cents a day, young Emma Tenayucca led the strikers' wives and daughters in setting up food kitchens for the men. Despite the violence women and men faced in the strike, they held out until they won a wage increase.

CHAPTER 18

INDUSTRIAL UNIONS FORM THE CIO

In 1935 of 30 million laborers in America only a tenth were in unions. Membership in the AFL had fallen from more than 4 million in 1918 to less than 3 million a decade later. In an age of mass production its leaders ignored the women and men who labored in mass production plants making steel, rubber, oil, textiles, planes, cars, and appliances. AFL leaders recruited only the most skilled elite of laborers, and this focus largely excluded women and people of color.

However, immigrant workers and their sons had been steadily rising into higher-paying, more respectable positions. In 1910 two-thirds of all immigrants were unskilled laborers, but by 1930, this proportion changed to less than half. In 1932 half of America's mill and mine workers were foreign-born, and few were in unions.

Mayor Fiorello La Guardia greets Pullman porters and their union leaders.

In 1928, A. Philip Randolph's Sleeping Car Porter's Union had half of all African Americans then in unions. The porter's union was admitted to the AFL, and every year Randolph stood at the AFL convention to demand the recruitment of African American workers. He also called for an end to union segregation and wanted to see the hiring of black organizers. Randolph's demands fell on deaf ears.

Then the stock market crash and the depression brought a rush of desperate workers of every background to unions. In 1933, 900,000 workers went on strike, triple the previous year, and 775,000 workers flocked to join unions. By the next year, a million and half went on strike.

In 1935 union membership received its first legislative protection with passage of the Wagner Labor Relations Act. Workers gained the right to join unions, and employers were prohibited from using unfair labor practices to disrupt unions.

John L. Lewis, president of the United Mine Workers (UMW), called for industrial unions that recruited everyone who worked in mines or mills regardless of his or her skills. His vice president, Philip Murray, launched an industrial union among steelworkers. Murray, born in Scotland in 1886, had arrived in the United States in 1902, began life as a coal miner, and became a UMW leader.

Philip Murray

In starting an industrial union, Murray was assisted by two Jewish immigrants, Sidney Hillman and David Dubinsky, who had earlier formed clothing unions. In 1907 at age 20 Hillman arrived in the U.S. from Lithuania and eventually became president of the Amalgamated Clothing Workers Union. Dubinsky, born in Russian-occupied Poland in 1892, spent time in a Siberian prison for organizing a baker's union. He escaped, reached the United States in 1911, and took work in the clothing industry. In 1932 he became president of the International Ladies Garment Workers and remained in that office until 1966.

Sidney Hillman

The United Auto Workers union was formed in 1935 under Walter Reuther. Reuther had been born in West Virginia to German immigrant parents.

In 1937 the AFL expelled the industrial unions of Lewis and Murray. Subsequently, 32 large and small unions met in 1938 at the first convention of the Congress of Industrial Organizations (CIO) and announced plans to organize "Negro or white, skilled or unskilled, men or women, American or foreign-born." Delegates unanimously called for a federal antilynching law and abolition of the poll tax that kept poor whites and Blacks in southern states from voting.

David Dubinsky

The first CIO recruiter in Detroit was assigned to locate the "nationalities" and hire organizers "who speak foreign languages." By 1937, Murray's organizers who could speak Polish, Serbian, Lithuanian, Russian, or Croatian had recruited thousands of steelworkers. In Detroit, Boleslaw Gebert, Stanley Nowak, and other Polish Americans used their paper *People's Voice*, to recruit men into the CIO's auto, steel and meat-packing unions.

Walter Reuther

In the steel industry where African Americans were 20 percent of the employees, Murray hired black organizers and announced that racial discrimination would not be tolerated. The NAACP, Urban League, and most African American ministers had resented white unions for their failure to enroll people of color. But now the CIO won their support. In Pittsburgh, Murray credited black organizer Benjamin Caruthers with signing up 2,000 workers and unionizing the huge steel mill at Aliquippa.

To organize black women, the CIO issued a pamphlet:

> Perhaps you are a Negro woman, driven to the worst part of town but paying the same high rent.... Your man is driven even harder than the white workers, but your man gets lower pay — hired the last and fired the first.... The remedy is to help the union. When it comes to exploitation, the mill owners draw no color line. The exploit the native white workers just as they do the Mexican, Polish, and Negro workers.

The CIO demanded equal rights for women and people of color. For this stand, CIO organizers faced violent attacks, and some lost their lives. Many corporations labeled them "Communists" and said that they acted under orders from Soviet Russia or American Communists.

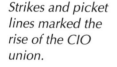

Strikes and picket lines marked the rise of the CIO union.

In 1935 less than 100,000 African Americans held union cards. Four years later half a million held union cards. Before 1936, African Americans rarely were elected to union posts, but after that date, black union officials became commonplace. In Pennsylvania a black CIO worker reported,

> The union is breaking down prejudice and segregation.... There is no office in the union that is held from a colored man because of his color.

NAACP legal authority Thurgood Marshall called the program of the CIO "the Bill of Rights for Negro labor in America."

In 1937 CIO unions began to stage sit-down strikes in which employees refused to leave their workplaces. In 8 months 485,000 women and men struck plants, offices, and department stores.

Rose Pesotta, who was born in 1896 in the Ukraine and migrated to the U.S. as a teenager, became a CIO organizer in Los Angeles, Seattle, Puerto Rico, Milwaukee, and Buffalo. In 1937 she helped lead the Akron, Ohio, women's auxiliary during a famous sit-down strike. She went on to organize Flint, Michigan, women in another sit-down strike.

Dorothy Bellanca, a Latvian immigrant, was an organizer for the Amalgamated Clothing Workers Union. Under organizers such as Pesotta and Bellanca, CIO men and women sang:

> When the boss won't talk, don't take a walk,
> Sit down! Sit Down!

Women's role in the CIO was celebrated in union songs. "The Union Maid" told of a woman who had no fear of violence and was ready "to organize the guys." The song concluded with this advice:

> You gals who want to be free, Just take a tip from me.
> Get yourself a union man and join the Ladies Auxiliary.

A mother passes her child to her husband during a 1938 sit-down strike in Flint, Michigan.

Women organize a sit-down strike.

AMERICANS CONFRONT THE MARCH OF FASCISM

During the Great Depression, Americans had to confront another disaster — the rise of Fascism and its threat to world peace. In the 1930s Fascist dictators — Hitler in Germany, Mussolini in Italy, and a Japanese military government — marched toward global war.

American bigots in the Ku Klux Klan, the Silver Shirts, the Christian Front, and the German American Bund felt encouraged by Nazi racism to attack the "Jew Deal" and President "Rosenfelt." Father Charles Coughlin, an Irish American priest, used his popular Sunday radio program to denounce Jews and to urge his Christian Front followers to arm for action. "I take the road of Fascism," he announced. Coughlin called financier Bernard Baruch and comedian Eddie Cantor "the two most dangerous Jews in America." Week after week people sent Coughlin more than $20,000 in contributions.

German Americans were divided about Hitler. Surveys showed that 70 percent of German Americans had no use for Nazism, and 21 percent were anti-Nazi. But 9 percent, including Charles Lindbergh, who in 1927 flew solo across the Atlantic to France, favored Hitler.

In 1933, 1,200 Yorkville, New York, German Americans met to sing Nazi songs and praise Hitler. Next Nazi agents tried to infiltrate and take over major German American groups. They failed to capture the Steuben Society, but their tactics wrecked many organizations. However, in 1934 Hitler's supporters in Yorkville boasted a Storm Trooper Corps and a Nazi Youth Corps.

By 1936, Fritz Kuhn's German American Bund united pro-Nazi forces. The Bund held rallies in Yorkville and ran a military training camp in New Jersey. An "American Nazi Party" the next year claimed 78 chapters with 200,000 members from Seattle, Washington, to Boston, Massachusetts. But this party and the Bund soon faded even in German American population centers such as Milwaukee, Wisconsin.

However, in February 1939, the Bund was able to draw 22,000 fans to a Madison Square Garden decked out with Nazi flags and uniformed American Nazis. When a Jewish New Yorker brashly tried to interrupt their meeting, he was pounced on by storm troopers. Soon after that, the major German American societies denounced the Kuhn, the Bund, and Nazism.

Jewish American war veterans were the first to call for a boycott of German products. They organized a massive rally that heard Mayor Fiorello La Guardia, Senator Wagner, and Walter White of the NAACP speak out against the Nazis.

African Americans were among the first citizens to see danger in Nazism. In 1933 black scholar Dr. Kelly Miller's article, "Hitler — The German Ku Klux," compared Nazi anti-Semitic attacks to the Klan attacks on Blacks in America. In 1935 the Nazi Nuremburg decrees, which were largely copied from racial segregation laws in the American South, banned Jews from German civil service and professional jobs. Mary McLeod Bethune's National Council of Negro Women was among the first to denounce the decree and to ask President Roosevelt to help Germany's Jews. In New York Vaughn Love's League of Struggle for Negro Rights said the Nuremburg Laws "meant death to us darker races" and said Fascism was "the enemy of all black aspirations."

Americans also reacted in October 1935, when Mussolini's Fascist troops marched into Ethiopia. African Americans raised funds and supplies to aid the Ethiopian government. In Chicago, African American Oliver Law planned a huge antifascist rally, but Mayor Kelly banned the meeting and sent 2,000 police to enforce his order. About 10,000 Chicago citizens arrived to demonstrate their opposition to Mussolini's invasion, and Law suddenly appeared on a rooftop to address the crowd. By the time police arrested him, another speaker spoke from another rooftop. Eventually six men spoke, and all six were arrested.

Oliver Law devoted his life to fighting injustice.

Hitler hoped the 1936 Olympics in Berlin would prove Nazi athletes were part of a "master race." Anti-Nazis organized an alternative Olympics in Barcelona, Spain, and invited athletes from all over the world.

Mr. Derounian's Mission

Born to Armenian parents in Greece in 1909, Arthur Derounian and his family fled Turkish persecution and arrived in the United States in 1921. Arthur always remembered his first Sunday in Mineola, Long Island:

> No Turks lurked around the corner. No corpses littered the streets. There was no need to hide in warehouses or cellars, to bolt the doors or talk in whispers. This was America. I was a gawky boy of 12 and so terrorized by past experiences I could hardly believe that one could live in one place any length of time without having to flee for safety.

Arthur's father told his children to "forget Europe." In 1926 Arthur became a citizen and graduated from New York University.

In 1938, Derounian was shocked to find some Americans handing out pro-Nazi leaflets. "I plunged into the opportunity to repay America in a humble way for her kindness and generosity." As George Pagnanelli, an alias Derounian adopted, he began to investigate those who sought to destroy "freedom in America."

Pagnanelli infiltrated dozens of Nazi and other hate groups. He discovered that "leaflets defaming Jews and Democracy" flowed into the United States from Nazi propaganda chief Joseph Goebbels' headquarters in Erfurt, Germany. "Pope Pius is a Jew" he was told by a man who sold anti-Catholic booklets.

Pagnanelli was told: "You got to create terror to get somewhere. You got to terrorize the Jews." He watched as storm troopers started fights. His concluded that "Hate was the Fascist formula" and that Nazism "dug at our flesh on many fronts."

Pagnanelli found groups which spoke for a "free America" but railed against foreigners, Jews, liberals, New Dealers, and Communists. Many of these groups had taken their ideas and gotten their money from Nazi Germany. Underground in the U.S. Fascist movement, the young investigator met senators, congressmen, and people from "old American families." He corresponded with leading Nazis in Germany.

In 1940 Pagnanelli was present when the German American Bund invited Christian Front and Ku Klux Klan leaders to their Camp Nordland in New Jersey. "The principles of the Bund and the principles of the Klan are the same," said a leader of the Nazi movement that day.

Pagnanelli found that pro-Nazi work did not stop after Pearl Harbor. In 1943 he exposed the pro-Nazi propaganda forces in a 544 page book. He wrote *Under Cover: My Four Years in the Nazi Underworld of America* using the pen name of John Roy Carlson. It alerted Americans to a hidden danger and became a best-seller. ■

At the Berlin Olympics African American Jesse Owens won four gold medals. But before Owens was awarded his medals, Hitler was rushed out of the stadium.

Race again became an issue in 1936 when Nazi boxing champion Max Schmeling knocked out Joe Louis, Detroit's "Brown Bomber." When Schmeling made insulting racial remarks about Louis before their next fight in 1938, the mild-mannered Louis became angry. Less than two minutes into the first round of a 15-round fight, Louis knocked out the representative of the "master race."

In New York City, Bill Bailey, a tall, young Irish American sailor, became increasingly upset by the news from Germany:

Schmeling and Louis weigh in for their 1938 heavyweight fight.

> Every week you would see Nazi storm troopers burning books, jailing people, laughing, and pushing old Jewish men and women to their knees to scrub streets with toothbrushes. One of those women could have been my mother!

On July 26, 1936 the German passenger liner *Bremen* was berthed in New York Harbor, a swastika flying from a mast. Bailey found his chance to strike back at Nazism when the *Bremen* offered sightseeing tours. Bailey, his buddy, "Low Life" McCormick, and some other seamen friends walked aboard as tourists.

While McCormick and the others battled the Nazi crew, Bailey tried to rip down the swastika, but it was stuck. "I would have eaten the thing to get it off," he said later. When it finally came loose, a howl went up, but Bailey and his friends were arrested. The police officer who took down their names looked up with surprise and said, "There ain't a Jew among them! They're all Irish!"

In the 1936 election Roosevelt carried every state but Maine and Vermont. A Union Party, backed by Father Coughlin which said it admired Hitler and Mussolini, drew fewer than a million votes.

During the American election campaign, Fascism continued its march in Europe. In July 1936 General Francisco Franco tried to overthrow the newly elected Republican government of Spain. Nazi and Italian planes ferried his troops from Morocco to Spain.

Men and women from all over the world, volunteered to save Spain from Fascism. Americans formed the Abraham Lincoln Brigade.

John Kozar, seaman.

American Evelyn Hutchins drove a truck in Spain during the civil war.

Franco's soldiers, aided by 50,000 Italian troops and the Nazi air force, marched on Madrid. Spain asked the world for help, and about 40,000 men and women from 54 nations rushed to its aid. For the first time in history a global volunteer force assembled to fight for democracy, "to make Madrid the tomb of world Fascism." Spanish poet Federico García Lorca left his studies at New York's Columbia University for Spain and died in the early fighting.

Some 2800 American volunteers calling themselves the Abraham Lincoln Brigade fought against Facism in Spain. Some were American athletes from the Barcelona Olympics.

More than half of the American volunteers had been born abroad or were sons and daughters of immigrants. One-third of the American volunteers were Jewish. "Nobody had to tell us Hitler was evil," one said.

Vaughn Love was one of many African Americans with Indian blood. Rudolpho de Armas, who came to America to escape the Batista dictatorship in Cuba, volunteered to prevent a Franco take-over. Herman Bottcher was a German who arrived in America from Australia. Jack Sharai, a Japanese citizen living in the United States, joined the Lincoln Brigade. John Kozar, a seaman, came from Europe by way of Canada. A few years before he had been jailed for smuggling guns to Germany's anti-Nazi underground.

Some 54 Lincoln Brigade volunteers were women, mostly nurses. But some, such as Evelyn Hutchins, won the right to drive trucks or ambulances. Marion Merriman, married to the first Lincoln Brigade commander, Captain Robert Merriman, was the only American woman officially listed as a soldier. "Spain," she said, "taught me how to live, how to value people."

The Lincoln Brigade included American Catholics, Protestants, Jews, atheists, Socialists, Communists, Republicans, and Democrats.

They came with enthusiasm and idealism and little military experience. Only a few had ever fired a gun. Victims of inexperience, many were wounded in their first days at the front.

One of the few with military experience was Oliver Law, who had 6 years in the 24th U.S. Infantry but could not rise above corporal because he was African American. In Spain, Law was appointed the Brigade commander and became the first African American in history to lead an integrated American fighting unit.

Jerry Weinberg and Oliver Law photographed together in 1937 before Law died in action.

The battlefields of Spain brought people together. Jerry Weinberg in New York and Oliver Law in Chicago had helped evicted families move back into their homes during the depression. In Spain they became best friends. At the Battle of Brunete, Weinberg crawled through enemy fire to carry back the mortally wounded Law. Walter Garland, an African American, was wounded as he crawled across the battlefield to rescue a dying Leo Kaufman he hardly knew.

Marc Haldane, son of a Native American from British Columbia, teamed up with Moishe Brier, a Brooklyn Jew, and Otto Reeves, the son of a African American minister from Cleveland. Irish American sailor Bill Bailey, Nick Pappas, a Greek American, and Luchelle McDaniels, an African American, became friends.

From left, Red Drummond, Nick Pappas, and Luchelle McDaniels.

Steve Nelson, born in Yugoslavia and an organizer for the jobless, became Brigade commander when Law died. In Chicago, Nelson and Law had been arrested for fighting racial discrimination and for demanding a federal unemployment insurance law.

Langston Hughes, Ernest Hemingway, and John Dos Passos came to Spain as journalists. James Yates drove Hughes to the war front where many African Americans in the Lincoln Brigade told the writer, "I never felt more like a man than I do in Spain." Paul Robeson sang for the Lincoln Brigade and other internationals.

The American volunteers hoped their courage and sacrifice would persuade the Western democracies that Fascism had to be stopped. But England, France, and the U.S. did nothing, and the Spanish Republic was defeated after 18 months of warfare. However, the Americans and the other international volunteers who survived the war felt their effort had slowed the Nazi war machine by 18 months.

Langston Hughes interviews Lincoln Brigader Crawford Morgan.

FURTHER READING

Adamic, Louis. *A Nation of Nations*. New York: Harper, 1944.

Barron, Milton, ed. *Minorities in a Changing World*. New York: Alfred A. Knopf, 1967.

Bernado, Stephanie. *The Ethnic Almanac*. New York: Dolphin, 1981.

Debo, Angie. *A History of the Indians of the United States*, rev. ed. Norman, OK: University of Oklahoma Press, 1984.

The Ethnic Chronology Series. Dobbs Ferry, NY: Oceana Publications, 1972-1990.

Evans, Sara M. *Born for Liberty: A History of Women in America*. New York: Macmillan, 1989.

Franklin, John Hope. *From Slavery to Freedom: A History of Negro Americans*, rev. ed. New York: Alfred A. Knopf, 1988.

The *In America* Series. Minneapolis, MN: Lerner Publications, 1971-1990.

Katz, William Loren. *The Invisible Empire: The Ku Klux Klan Impact on History*. Seattle, WA: Open Hand Publications, 1988.

Millstein, Beth and Bodin, Jeanne, eds. *We, the American Women: A Documentary History*. New York: Ozer Publishing, 1977.

Moquin, Wayne, ed. *A Documentary History of the Mexican Americans*. New York: Praeger, 1972.

Seller, Maxine S. *To Seek America: A History of Ethnic Life in the United States*. Englewood, NJ: Ozer Publishing, 1977.

Shannon, William V. *The American Irish*. New York: Macmillan, 1964.

Takaki, Ronald. *Strangers from a Different Shore: A History of Asian Americans*. New York: Penguin Books, 1990.

Thernstrom, Stephan, ed. *Harvard Encyclopedia of American Ethnic Groups*. Cambridge, MA: Belknap Press, 1980.

INDEX